THE READER'S EYE

Robert L. Montgomery

The Reader's Eye

*Studies in Didactic Literary Theory
from Dante to Tasso*

University of California Press
Berkeley · Los Angeles · London

University of California Press
Berkeley and Los Angeles, California
University of California Press, Ltd.
London, England
ISBN 0-520-03700-6
Library of Congress Catalog Card Number 78-57313

Contents

Acknowledgments

Several people read my manuscript in various stages. They are: Hazard Adams, James Chiampi, Ralph Friedman, O. B. Hardison, Jr., Murray Krieger, and Harold Toliver. I am more than grateful for their informed and helpful advice, and I value the encouragement they have given.

I wish to acknowledge the helpfulness of the staffs of the British Library and the Henry E. Huntington Library, where most of my reading was done. In addition, my thanks to the Huntington for permission to use its copies of the following books for quotation and reference: Castelvetro, *Poetica d'Aristotile*; Fracastoro, *Opera Omnia*; Mazzoni, *Della Difesa della Commedia di Dante*; and Tasso, *Discorsi del Arte Poetica*.

Finally, I am grateful to Mrs. Mary Gazlay and Mrs. Doris Merrifield for swift and accurate typing.

Introduction

This book examines the work of five didactic theorists beginning with Dante in the early fourteenth century and continuing with Fracastoro, Daniele Barbaro, Sidney, and Tasso in the Renaissance. I have brought these figures together for close scrutiny (and relegated some others to briefer comment) in order to emphasize a mode of didacticism which gives unusual prominence to questions of audience response, thereby forcing the argument for the teaching function of literature beyond conventional piety and beyond the usual attention to such matters as the poet's knowledge or character and the techniques, forms, and doctrines with which he is concerned. What we have, I believe, is a kind of didactic theory which seeks to explain or defend the value of fiction primarily in terms of the ends it gains in the mind of the reader and ultimately in his moral behavior.

These ends are implicit in most didactic criticism stretching from passages in Aristophanes' *The Frogs* to well beyond the Renaissance, but they are seldom made explicit or demonstrated with the thoroughness shown by Dante and his successors. In broad outline the central

propositions of didacticism are familiar: the main functions of the poetic text are understood to be the teaching
of certain kinds of truth, either propositions to be
accepted by rational assent or standards of conduct to be
grasped and followed. Companion to these is the belief
that literature must be pleasing, and pleasure is usually
considered the means by which truth is made palatable.
The didactic theorist is inclined to see the poet's role and
the formal properties of his work as dependent in one
way or another upon these requirements, though occasionally the results of the poem are treated as a mere
by-product of form and thus not essential to definitions
of literary art. Most didactic theory gives primary weight
to questions of doctrine and technique. Horace's *Art of
Poetry*, for example, deals mostly in formal matters, and
the same is true of such standard Renaissance texts as
Vida's *De Arte Poetica*, Minturno's *De Poeta*, and Scaliger's *Poetices*. Most modern studies of pre-Romantic
literary theory have echoed these priorities.[1]

My intention is different. I focus on texts that propose
or use a developed psychology of audience response and
argue in detail the influence of fiction and fictive images
on the passions, imagination, intellect, and will. This
psychology and the power it grants to language in a
fictional context is frequently mentioned or assumed in
early critical texts and in treatises on oratory and rhetoric. In Plotinus and in Proclus's commentaries on Plato,
as well as in Longinus,[2] there are interesting discussions
that point up some connections between fictional language and the capacities of the mind to receive them.
But in Dante's *Vita Nuova* and especially in the *Purgatorio*
one notices for the first time a sustained effort to
demonstrate the impact of art upon the affective powers

and its subsequent influence over the will. Dante's absorption in both theology and poetics led him to supplement doctrine with a close interest in the ways in which art (both plastic and verbal) can modify the condition of the soul, and although it would be quite wrong to suggest that his example had a direct influence upon didactic theories in the Renaissance, there is a steady continuation of similar interests noticeable in the critical writings of Boccaccio, Petrarch, and the fifteenth-century Humanists (especially Coluccio Salutati), as well as in the general concern of Humanism for the persuasive and educative functions of language.[3] But while Dante looks at the affective motives of art in the context of the soul's movement towards salvation and a vision of the divine, later versions of didactic and affective theory are pointed at the consequences of art for moral behavior. In this context poetry is viewed not as an aid to salvation or contemplation, but as an incitement to virtuous conduct in this life. As the maker of fictions the poet must also be the agent of moral truth and his images must be such that they move the sensibility of the audience to act upon that truth. For the critic attentive to their implications such imperatives raise two fundamental questions: In what way does the literary image, which is by definition sensory and particular, permit the mind's access to general or universal truths that have no material being? And how do the faculties of the mind respond to such images?

Both questions are bound into the ways in which the didactic critic frames his concept of the audience. For the period of time and the critical texts under review here the concept of the audience leans on Aristotelian faculty psychology, and within that tradition of psychology it is

the concept of the imagination which is of greatest
interest to the critic. For this reason I devote chapter one
to a discussion of certain moments in the history of
faculty psychology and the ways in which it describes
the imagination. Pre-Romantic notions of the creative, or
poet's imaginative powers have enjoyed some modern
notice, especially in the writings of Murray W. Bundy
and Baxter Hathaway, and these are useful in charting
the traffic between theories of poetic invention and
traditional faculty psychology.[4] However, to gain some
sense of what powers were supposed to be available to
the literary audience, we must look again at this body of
thought with somewhat different motives. What is at
issue is neither the creative visionary imagination of the
Romantic critics nor the "higher" inventive power that a
recent critic discerns behind Spenser's allegory.[5] We are
dealing instead with a more mundane, though vital
power, a capacity that according to Aristotle and most of
his successors in the Middle Ages belongs to the sensitive soul. At this subrational level imagination is the
faculty of turning sense impressions, or their surrogates,
into mental pictures, of reproducing within the mind,
even in the absence of the original impression, the
images of material things. It is also a faculty that can
combine images. These processes of picturing allow the
mind to retain, recall, modify, and respond to objects
that have lost their material being but function as if they
had not. The imagination thus construed is fluid, change-
able, vivid, and often wayward; it is irrational as well as
nonrational, and yet it is essential to all mental and
emotional life. Believed to be the agent of affective
response (i.e., desire or aversion), it is also supposed to
provide the material on which the reason dwells or the

means by which it speculates. In other words imagination is the necessary precondition for both feeling and thought, and if the images of literary or artistic fictions have some relation to the material or natural world, then a belief in this mediating imagination is most useful, if not essential, to the critic who wants to describe the nature of the audience and its response. Chapter One will serve, therefore, as a prelude to what such critics are up to.

In chapter two I examine some of Dante's writings, especially passages in the *Vita Nuova* and *Purgatorio* which testify to his experience of the affective and reformative powers of art. In the company of Renaissance critics Dante may seem anomalous, for he precedes the major phase of Humanist thinking by more than a century and the full maturity of Renaissance literary theory by two centuries. I might add that I find his most interesting thinking about art in his poems, and so must do them the partial injustice of treating them as documents in the history of theory. Finally, his poetic, dependent as it is upon doctrines of grace and inspiration, varies in these respects from the more secular thinking of later critics. Yet in striking ways he anticipates the later writers with whom I deal, especially in his accounts of the influence of art upon the imagination and will. On the terraces of Purgatory Dante exemplifies the spectator of art, just as he exemplifies and acts out the progress of the human soul, so that the record of his response becomes a paradigm for a general theory of the reception of art in the mind. This narrows the distance between what Dante acts out and, for example, the moving power Sidney attributes to the poetic image.

Those after Dante whom I have chosen to treat in

detail participate in many of the larger critical concerns
of the Renaissance, but they have the special virtue of
exhibiting a fairly steady line of affective criticism which
avoids the extremes of Neoplatonic or Aristotelian dogma. They view poetic invention and poetic form primarily from the standpoint of the requirements of teaching,
persuading, and moving, and they consciously refer to
the tradition of Aristotelian faculty psychology. Chapter
three takes up Giralomo Fracastoro and Daniele Barbaro.
Three of Fracastoro's works—the dialogues entitled
Naugerius, *Turrius*, and *Fracastorius* (all first printed in
1555, though composed somewhat earlier)—deal re-
spectively with poetry, the intellect, and the soul. Together these dialogues provide the most thorough inquiry into the processes of thought of any of the works I
discuss, and they combine most precisely a theory of the
nature of the poetic image with a fully articulated
account of the processes of perception and generaliza-
tion. Barbaro's *Della Eloquenza* (1557) examines the impact and value of art by fashioning a colloquy between
Nature, Soul, and Art which defines the ways in which
literary images combine the sensible and the intellectual,
so that the reader may gain, through the agency of the
image, some glimpse of the unseen.

Chapter four is a study of Sidney's *Apology for Poetry*,
composed in the early 1580s and published in two
versions in 1595. This is perhaps the most widely familiar of all theoretical essays written in the Renaissance. It
synthesizes many of the insights of Sidney's Italian
predecessors (among them Fracastoro, from whom he
borrowed much) and restates them in the context of an
unusually emphatic argument for the positive affective

value of poetic fiction. The "defensive" mode of theory, begun by Boccaccio, finds its most complete and powerful expression in Sidney, and perhaps also its most distinctive, for it is important to realize that Sidney's case rests as much upon the appeal of fiction to sense and imagination as it does upon confidence in the poet's moral doctrine, inventive freedom, or the reader's "upright wit."

Tasso's *Discourses on the Heroic Poem* (1594) is the subject of chapter five. As with the others, his theory continues to argue a didactic final cause for poetry, but in a different context. Tasso is self-consciously sensitive to diverse critical systems. Where Fracastoro and Sidney could without any sense of strain urge the poet's liberty of invention, Tasso reacts to and accepts a fairly stern Aristotelian insistence on mimetic credibility, verisimilitude, and the need for grounding the poetic fable in history. These requirements, as Tasso defines them, impose a substantially different and more restricted view of what in the poetic fable will be persuasive, and this is directly related to his sense of an audience whose attitudes are conditioned by their own history and Christian culture. He is thus led to conceive a kind of poem unlike those made in pre-Christian times, and he thus also brings to a close the mode of didacticism with which I am occupied. For Dante, Fracastoro, Barbaro, Sidney, and others like them, the audience is virtually universal, responding with common faculties to the timeless images and enduring values of conduct in poetic forms themselves exempt from local custom or historical peculiarity. Without entirely abandoning these positions, Tasso nevertheless begins their qualification when he points up the differences between the literature of the past and that which could be persuasively composed in his own time.

In the choice of these writers my procedure is, of course, selective, rather than exhaustive or comprehensive. Nor do I maintain that the issues central to their theories make a fresh and sudden appearance in the early fourteenth century or disappear with the end of the sixteenth. Instead I think we can see between these dates a pattern of consistency and coherence which is not so clear either before or after, an articulate gathering of psychology, persuasive motive, and formal speculation whose outlines finally dissolve in the new combinations that interested theorists in the seventeenth century. My intent, then, is to offer a concentrated look at one kind of critical thought without suggesting that it is necessarily sealed off in time or in doctrine from neighboring concerns.

Two of these concerns are especially relevant—I refer to the traditions of oratorical (and rhetorical) criticism and the modes of reading which understood fiction as allegory. Because both have benefited from substantial modern commentary, I offer only summary attention here to point up some of the ways they overlap and are involved with didacticism. I shall deal with oratory and rhetoric first.

Theories of oratory and theories of literature remained distinct disciplines in antiquity and the Middle Ages, but they borrowed liberally from each other. Horace's *Art of Poetry*, for example, shows the influence of a number of topics familiar in Ciceronian oratorical doctrine. Central to both are their analogous designs upon the audience, which naturally invite attention to the responsive faculties. The poet's need to compel the feelings of his readers; the requirement that he offer valid images to cater to the human delight in imitation; and his habit of appealing through harmony and rhythm to the taste for verbal music—all these have their counterparts in oratorical theory.[6] Moreover, poetry and rhetoric were understood to share a relationship to moral philosophy, sometimes as two of the instrumental modes of ethics.[7] These common purposes and associations survived to be rethought and reargued during the growth of Humanist concepts of education in the fifteenth century, and the vigorous attention such figures as Boccaccio, Petrarch, and Salutati gave to the arts of discourse fed directly into sixteenth century literary theory. The parallel and often overlapping interests of the two disciplines guaranteed an enduring and powerful rhetorical focus to literary theory, and it is worth remarking that all of the Renaissance texts I discuss in detail make use of the inherited association between poetry and oratory. They are concerned as well with the ties of poetry to moral philosophy as the source of the doctrine that the literary audience must be persuaded to embrace.

If we turn to the long tradition of allegorical interpretation, we discover another mode of relationships between poetry, oratory, and philosophy. Where literary and oratorical theory share a concern for persuasive motives and means, literary theory and the conventions of allegorical interpretation jointly focus on the relationship between the fictional image and doctrine. From one point of view the poetic fable is a form of concealment. In Boccaccio's words it "veils truth in a fair and fitting garment of fiction."[8] And as Hardison notes, the widespread habit of allegorical criticism allows poetry to be classified with philosophy more explicitly than with rhetoric,[9] though in practical terms poetry was still seen to have a great deal in common with rhetoric throughout the Middle Ages and Renaissance. When we consider the question of the poetic audience, however, it is evident that the tradition of allegorical reading points in two rather different directions. If allegory is understood to veil and conceal, then a learned and restricted audience is required for interpretation. Boccaccio meets this issue by postulating two audiences for the same work: fiction "pleases the unlearned by its external appearance, and exercises the minds of the learned with its hidden truth; and thus both are edified and delighted with one and the same perusal."[10]

These remarks suggest that allegory is purposely designed to stretch the capacities of a learned audience, but medieval critics also recognized that some kinds of truth were resistant to any other form of expression. Boccaccio concedes that "some things are naturally so profound that not without difficulty can the most exceptional keenness in intellect sound their depths. . . ."[11] Where allegory is of this kind it tends to move poetry away from oratory. Indeed according to Michael Murrin, "The allegorical poet affects his audience more in the manner of a Hebrew prophet than in that of a classical orator."[12] The Renaissance example that comes most immediately to mind is Giordano Bruno's *Heroic Frenzies*, a textbook in the theory and practice of arcane allegorical symbolism, but the sixteenth-century critics most thoroughly committed to didacticism are inclined to stress not the difficulty of the fable or image, but its perspicuity and persuasiveness. And allegory was by no means altogether or always thought of as an obscuring medium. It was frequently seen as a way of representing general concepts and of bringing them into focus through the medium of example. For instance, in Hardison's view, "example naturally tends to develop into allegory."[13] Example also tends to take the form of picture, that is of events and characters that verbally embody ideas or propositions and that may be visualized in the mind of the reader.[14] Whether allegory in this mode is considered a separate kind or simply one of the several levels on which complex fiction may be interpreted, it is understood to clarify rather than to obscure, to make the conceptual familiar rather than mysterious or prophetic. By drawing poetry and oratory closer in their means and ends this line of thinking about allegory presumably requires little or no distinction between images that delight and those that have significance, and so there would be less inclination to distinguish among learned and ignorant audiences. Allegory as an informing and perspicuous kind of fiction is mentioned by Fracastoro, Barbaro, Sidney, and Tasso, but their didactic theories do not by any means attempt to argue that all instructive fiction is allegorical. With the partial exception of Tasso, they are committed to the usefulness and the delightfulness of all fiction, and they are, for the most part, interested in a broadly defined audience.

These commitments involve a steady emphasis on picture, on the sensible and particular in literature, as well as on example. Each term has certain implications: *picture* suggests an appeal to the mind through the senses and imagination, while *example* reminds us that

images, incidents, and characters were understood as
intended to point to general or universal considerations.
This is as much as to repeat that in the didactic theories
we have in view the governing motive is to think of
fiction according to the ways it may influence the audience, both affectively and intellectually. The fictional
image is designed to mediate between the faculties of a
more or less general audience and those abstract or
general truths whose value is already conceded. By
these standards literature is thought to be at once
compelling and morally useful, and those elements in it
which may copy or reflect the particulars of material
nature or human action are required also to embody
what is beyond or behind the particular. It should be
added that Renaissance critics who thought this way
also conceded that abstract or general truth can be
expressed by precept instead of example, by philosophy
instead of poetry, but this, as Sidney argued, would rob
truth of its capacity to move the will. The poet, he
reminds us, is "the right popular philosopher," a phrase
that brings us back to the audience and its needs as the
consideration that gives poetry its dignity and status: the
aim is common moral education. Even Spenser, in some
respects the most complex of prophetic poets, informed
Raleigh that instead of employing "good discipline delivered plainly by way of precepts," he had shaped his
art to the temper of the times, "seeing all things are
accounted by their showes, and nothing esteemed of,
that is not delightfull and pleasing to commune sence."[15]

I

Faculty Psychology and Theories of Imagination: Aristotle, Plato, Augustine, and Aquinas

In this chapter I offer a selective review of some elements in the history of faculty psychology to remind us of concepts of mental function which Dante and his successors found plausible. My account is necessarily summary. It passes over most of the issues that divided Stoics, Scholastics, Neoplatonists, or Averroists. Such distinctions were of little interest to the literary theorist whose main concerns centered on the fictional image and its appeal to the powers of the mind. This means that our attention to faculty psychology deals first with what is said about the way images mediate between sense perception and deliberative reasoning, and second with speculation about the role of imaginative experience in stimulating the feelings. How these issues are handled helps explain the importance of faculty psychology to the literary theorist, for the most serious obstacle to justifying literature as an intellectually and morally responsible form of discourse is the charge that it misleads men as to the truth—that it encourages idleness and lasciviousness or is simply frivolous.

The didactic theorist tends to deny such charges directly, arguing that the lies of poetry can be read sententiously and that even the poet's concern with the sensory and emotional—both in what he depicts and in the quality of his style—may give benefit in their power to affect the reader. Imaginative literature must also bear conviction, and its apologist must be able simultaneously to point out its doctrinal values and its persuasive force. This, as Quintillian's account of a commonplace suggests, is why artful language is preferable to unadorned precept: "Nay, even the principles which should guide our life, however fair they may be by nature, yet have greater power to mould the mind to virtue, when the beauty of things is illumined by the splendor of eloquence."[1] The audience must be led to rational assent in such a way that perception and appetite are moved in the direction wanted by the author. Virtuous behavior, which the mode of didacticism we are to study believes to be the poet's ultimate goal, is, as Aristotle had pointed out, the ordering of man's irrational nature.[2] Therefore the poet's task is to reach and influence the faculties of his audience so as to guide behavior, and his task may be more ambitious and difficult than that of the orator or rhetorician because his medium is language in an invented or fictional context. For the didactic theorist the need to explain the positive use of un-truth becomes a matter of some urgency.

As I have suggested in the introduction, these imperatives contain the logic according to which some critics explored the nature of the mind of the audience through a resort to faculty psychology, and especially through those of its elements which describe the imagination and its functions. Imagination, more than any other power of the mind, was thought to be the agency through which images—the data of perception—reached the higher faculties and by which, at the same time, the feelings were aroused. The critical tradition of linking the images of fiction and the plastic arts to detailed accounts of the mind's response begins to be expressed maturely in Dante, although there is an earlier and rather different effort in the writings of Proclus.[3] And Dante, like his successors, discovered in the sort of commentary on the nature of the soul which has its origins in Aristotle and Plato those features of psychology necessary to his theory. What Artistotle and Plato had to offer was colored and modified by later philosophical and theological discussion, especially by the efforts of Christian philosophy to come to terms with fallen man's ability to establish contact with divine as well as natural truth. It is also the case that the post-classical struggle with these issues was carried on with minimal reference to fiction or the plastic arts. Even so, the views of the mind which grew out of early psychology remained broadly constant and eventually serviceable to didactic literary theory.

ARISTOTLE AND PLATO

The seminal and dominant voice in the history of faculty psychology is Aristotle's. His is the first attempt at a systematic psychology, and subsequent thinkers, even those who were otherwise more dependent upon Platonic or other systems of philosophy, were inclined to turn to his account of the mind's faculties and functions. These had, of course, been discussed by Plato, but in a somewhat special context: some account of Plato is necessary to understand doubts about sensory and imaginative perception which had to be answered. But Augustine (whose emphasis upon the will is echoed in Humanist thinking) reflects with some qualification a basically Aristotelian understanding of mental function, and Scholastic philosophers revived and sophisticated Aristotle's interest in the processes of knowledge and established the versions of Aristotelian psychology in general use in the Renaissance. Accordingly, I begin with Aristotle.

The *De Anima* can be read as an attempt to explore the coordination of human consciousness and nature, to describe the ways in which sensing, feeling, and thinking are responsive to our material environment, as well as the ways in which the mind can go beyond matter. For Aristotle all sentient and conscious life is movement, that is, a reaction in time to impressions on the mind from outside. In such a context the imagination is first of all a faculty central to the mind's ability to organize sense impressions so that they become either the objects of knowledge or the instruments of thought. Aristotle's metaphor for imagination relates to seeing and to light: "As sight is the most highly developed sense, the name *phantasia* (Imagination) has been formed from *phaos* (light) because it is not possible to see without light" (*De Anima* 429a). As a faculty of the sensitive (not the rational) soul, imagination is the inner counterpart of sense perception and is dependent upon images developed through the working of the outer senses. "Imagination," Aristotle says, "must be a movement resulting from an actual exercise of the power of sense" (428b). It is also, he notes, a power common to all animals, an ability to recreate within the mind those impressions that are no longer immediately before the organs of sense. There is thus a close connection between Aristotle's basic definition of imagination and a concept of memory, a connection necessary to the continuation of active, conscious life, for without the ability to retain and recall the images of sensory experiences, each impression would be unique, distinct, disconnected, and therefore unfathomable. So the dependence of the imagination on the recollection of sense images—especially those produced by seeing—is what allows the rational powers of the mind to work in an extended and systematic way on its experience of the material world. Whatever else later thinkers might say about the imagination, they could not entirely ignore this fundamental link between matter and mind.

The pages Aristotle devotes to the imagination belong to a more general inquiry into processes of thinking related to perception.[4] Concerned to mark off the stages by which the mind goes from registering particular facts about its material environment to classifying and judging them, he says that imagination with the help of memory is the crucial transition between animal response and deliberative reasoning. Imagination resembles perception on the one hand and reasoning on the other, but it is identical with neither. Like perception it sees images; like reason it can function at will. Above all it provides the material for thought: "To the thinking soul images serve as if they were the contents of perception. . . . That is why the soul never thinks without an image" (431a). The second assertion echoes almost unfailingly through the pages of later works on the nature of the mind; even those who did not share Aristotle's belief that the objects of sense are the true content of thought had to find a way around it.

Nevertheless, for Aristotle certain functions of thought had to be distinguished from imagining. First of all, thinking and perceiving are different because perceiving is automatically accurate, "while it is possible to think falsely as well as truly." In this sense imagination is not free to choose. At the same time, imagination is not the same as opinion (or judgment) because opinion involves guesswork, belief, conviction, and reasoning. Opinion, according to Aristotle, is equivalent to value judgment, while imagination is the revisualizing of something previously perceived. It may be a false re-creation, but it is not a false opinion of what is seen: "But what we imagine is sometimes false though our contemporaneous judgment about it is true: e.g. we imagine the sun to be a foot in diameter though we are convinced that it is larger than the inhabited part of the earth" (428a-428b). At this level imagination is capable of only a limited sort of judgment, that involved in the identification of physical properties. "I mean," Aristotle says, "that imagination must be the blending of the perception of white with the opinion that it is white: it could scarcely be a blend of the opinion that it is good with the perception that it is white" (428a). Imagination can decide physical properties; judgment is required for a decision about value.

The imagination is also more than a bridge between sense impressions and knowledge or understanding, for mental processes usually imply action, and action is accompanied by appetite. In making his distinction between direct sense perception and imagination, he notes our awareness of objects present to the senses: "when we think something to be fearful or threatening, emotion is immediately produced, and so too with what is encouraging; but when we merely imagine we remain as unaffected as persons who are looking at a painting of some dreadful or encouraging scene" (427b). The apparent affective weakness of imaginative presentations in relation to direct sense presentations bears upon Aristotle's concept of literary affect, and this can be clarified somewhat by reference to other treatises. In *De Somniis* he notes that "even when the external object of perception has departed, the impressions it has made persist, and are themselves objects of perception. . . ."[5] Later in *De Anima* he makes a similar point: "but sometimes by virtue of the images or thoughts which are within the soul, just as if it were seeing, it calculates and deliberates what is to come by reference to what is present; and when it makes a pronouncement, as in the case of sensation, it pronounces the object to be pleasant or painful . . ." (431b). Such reactions depend in part upon Aristotle's concept of the double status of images in the imagination or in paintings: "A picture painted on a panel is at once a picture and a likeness: that is, while one and the same, it is both of these, although the 'being' of both is not the same, and one may contemplate it either as a picture, or as a likeness. Just in the same way we have to conceive that the mnemonic presentation within us is something which by itself is

merely an object of contemplation, while, in relation to
something else, it is also a presentation of that other
thing."[6] In other words, it is possible to react to a
remembered image as if it were an immediate sensation,
but if we react to it as a likeness our emotion may be
weaker or different.

Imagination, though not precisely the source or organ
of emotion, is closely involved with it: imagination and
appetite combine to produce emotion. Imagination alone
may not engender emotion: "The mind often thinks
about something without enjoining the emotion of fear."
On the other hand appetite alone is not enough, for
sometimes the mind inhibits the following of appetite.
Joined they account for the "movement" of appetite,
and it is at this point that Aristotle approaches describing imagination almost as a kind of thinking: ". . . many
men follow their imaginations contrary to knowledge"
(433a).

Two problems have now been raised: If imagination
differs from sense perception in part because of its
relative weakness of affect, how is it that imagination
and appetite may function together? And if imagination
is confined to the recovery or reproduction of sense
impressions, how can it project or conceive what is not
present so that we can say that men follow their imaginations sometimes? In one place Aristotle suggests that
wish can stimulate appetite (434a), and in another he
says that if imagination precedes desire by presenting to
the mind a desirable object, then appetite can be said to
be stimulated by mind, especially if the imagining is
accompanied by opinion (433a). We may perhaps find
some clarification in a passage from *De Rhetorica* in

which Aristotle is attempting to explain the impact of verbal imagery: ". . . pleasure is the consciousness through the senses of a certain kind of emotion; but imagination is a feeble sort of sensation, and there will always be in the mind of a man who remembers or expects something an image of what he remembers or expects. If this be so, it is clear that memory and expectation also, being accompanied by sensation, may be accompanied by pleasure. It follows that anything pleasant is either present and perceived, past and re-membered, or future and expected. . . . Now the things that are pleasant to remember are not only those that, when actually perceived as present, *were* pleasant, but also some things that were not, provided that their results have subsequently proved noble and good. . . ."[7] This is one way to account for the pleasure we may take in certain kinds of artistic representation; it is also, since we may infer that the same mental complex may pro-duce distressing emotions, a way of accounting for the stimulation of appetite in general in the absence of an immediate object. Imagination thus continues to operate as a surrogate for sense impressions under certain conditions.

If we return now to *De Anima*, we find Aristotle also suggesting a higher or at least different mode of imagin-ing, the "deliberative" or calculative, which is more or less a function of the practical reason.[8]

Sensitive imagination, as we have said, is found in all animals, deliberative imagination only in those that are calculative: for whether this or that shall be enacted is already a task requiring calculation; and there must be a single standard to measure by, for that is pursued which is *greater*. It follows that what acts in this way must be able to make a unity out of several images. (434a)[9]

The deliberative reason, which I take to be that mental function by which we plan our actions, thus uses the imagination to provide images in a context. If imagination offers images in such a way that they may be compared or judged not as single or isolated impressions but as composites of some kind, this may help explain how both the reason and the appetite can pursue objects that are not simply material but have some status as ideas.

Aritstotle thus offers several concepts that were to become useful to didactic and affective criticism. First, imagination is established as a kind of mental picturing that precedes and makes possible opinion and judgment about objects and their images; it borders on reasoning but is not to be absolutely equated with it. Second, it is related to appetite and emotion by providing them with objects in the absence of immediate sense impression. We can feel at a distance, as it were, though such a reaction to pictures in the mind is neither inevitable nor automatic. Opinion and judgment permit us to contemplate an image either with a relative lack of desire or aversion or with responses different from those the immediate object would provoke (as in *Poetics* 1448b), but there is also a kind of relationship between imagination and appetite when an image is sufficiently attractive to the will. Third, there is a mode of imagining in which constituted or "invented" images become the counters of thought, and here too there appears to be in men the possibility of moving the will, sometimes in a way that defeats reason.

Plato's notorious distrust of poetry as an organ of truth and his attitude towards the experience of the senses nevertheless open up the possibility that the imagination is crucial to artistic creation, and his insistence on the human tendency to imagine falsely engendered later speculation about the ability of the mind to register more than sensible forms. For Plato what the senses perceive are appearances, and although they may to some degree imitate realities, these appearances are always at least partially false. Essential truth is disembodied and independent of what is phenomenal and material. For Aristotle the task of the intellect is to reason and generalize about the phenomenal world or about matters derived from observation; as a result his psychology proposes an orderly movement of the mind from perceived image to rationally contemplated idea. Plato, for the most part, seems to regard images, especially those born of the direct perception of phenomena, as impediments to proper intellection. Therefore his notion of mental function is somewhat different. Since for him the intellectual and the phenomenal are distinct, and often opposed, he offers a theory of the faculties which divides instead of harmonizes their functions.

This division is apparent at the end of Book VI of the *Republic* where Socrates attempts to explain to Glaucon what the separation of the intellectual and visible worlds means. Socrates illustrates his point by supposing that a line is to be divided into two unequal parts, one representing the intellectual and the other the visible. He then supposes that the two divisions be subdivided. The line representing the visible is thus separated into images, which he terms "shadows" or reflections in water or on polished surfaces, and the visible things they represent.

Arguing that these subdivisions have "different degrees of truth, and that the copy is to the original as the sphere of opinion is to the sphere of knowledge," he maintains that the mind uses the image or shadow as a "hypothesis" by which to arrive at some knowledge of the object. In a parallel manner, knowledge of the intellectual world is also approached hypothetically, the reasoning of dialectic being the counterpart to the use of images. Thus the mind uses hypotheses "not as first principles [but] as steps and points of departure into a world which is above hypotheses, in order that she may soar beyond them to the first principle of the whole; and clinging to this and then to that which depends on this, by successive steps she descends again without the aid of any sensible object, from ideas, through ideas, and in ideas she ends" (510–511).

Socrates' distinction between types of thinking is based on a scale of clarity. Dialectic, in reaching for "knowledge and being," employs hypotheses instrumentally and temporarily. The arts, although they too employ hypotheses, are contemplated by the understanding, not the reason, and the understanding, whose operation is indicated by the geometer's use of lines and angles, is midway between opinion and reason in the scale of clarity. Book VI concludes with a scale of faculties corresponding to the four divisions of objects: "Let there be four faculties in the soul—reason answering to the highest, understanding to the second, faith (or conviction) to the third, and perception of shadows to the last—and let there be a scale of them, and let us suppose that the several faculties have clearness in the same degree that their objects have truth."[10]

Plato limits reason and understanding to the world of

ideas, and faith (presumably what Aristotle calls opinion) and perception (probably imagination but not so termed here) to the world of objects, and this categorization flows from his belief that only the realm of ideas has reality or truth. The phenomenal world, which stands between the mind and its perception of truth, is at best a distorted reflection of something fixed and permanent, so that what the senses and imagination and opinion know is error.

Aristotle supposes that the imagination is capable of both accuracy and error, but he argues that a false image in the mind is nevertheless a psychological fact. Plato also seems to acknowledge a capacity for accurate reproduction—I refer to the discussion of icastic and phantastic imitation in the *Sophist* (235–236, 264–267). Icastic imitation is the accurate "mimicry" of things that exist, or in other terms "that which coexists with science" (267). Phantastic imitation is the copying of appearances, and in linking imagination to sense and opinion (264), Plato relegates those arts such as drawing, painting, and sculpture to the realm of phantastic imitation.[11] This kind of imitation or image-making always produces distortions: an imitation such as a work of art *must* be inaccurate in order to *appear* accurate to the spectator whose perspective, if we are talking simply of physical accuracy, prevents him seeing an object in its true dimensions. Plato extends this argument to the realm of thought so that he comes up with an attitude towards sense and imagination very much like that in Book X of the *Republic* where the artist or poet is characterized as an imitator at three removes from the truth. "The imitator or maker of the image knows nothing of true existence; he knows appearances only" (*Republic* 601).

Where the maker (the artisan) at least has belief but not knowledge, the imitator has neither, and his works are directed to the irrational faculties in his audience: "As in a city when the evil are permitted to have authority and the good are put out of the way, so in the soul of man, as we maintain, the imitative poet implants an evil constitution, for he indulges the irrational nature which has no discernment of greater and less, but thinks the same thing at one time great and at another small—he is a manufacturer of images and is very far removed from the truth" (*Republic* 605).

If we try to anticipate what the two quite diverse and even opposed positions of Aristotle and Plato might mean for later critical theory, we can at least speculate that an Aristotelian concept of the imagination would permit the reader to accommodate verbal images as accurate translations of the phenomenal world and suitable for rational contemplation and generalizing, while Plato's view would reduce the audience to an affective level below opinion. Presumably any kind of judgment of truth on the part of the artistic audience is impossible. Taken without elaboration, Aristotle's view of imagination would allow the audience to understand images as copies of existing things and as analogically related to universal concepts; on the same terms Plato's view would condemn the audience to the literal acceptance of fictions or lies.[12] Yet later critics had somehow to believe that the reader's mind was capable of grasping literary imagery as the author meant it to be understood, and this intention had to accommodate both the mimetic function and the task of making the phenomenal translate and communicate the intellectual. Plato's denigration of sense experience, if taken too much to heart, would make the allowance of any positive value to literature and art at best problematic, simply because they are in one form or another made up of sensory images.

A measure of the Platonic influence is available in the theories of Proclus, the third century A.D. commentator on Plato. Largely ignoring the *Republic*, especially Book X, Proclus seeks to dignify some kinds of poetry by reference to concepts of inspiration in *Ion* and the *Phaedrus*. As Hardison says, "the approach is if not a conscious distortion—an egregious case of special pleading."[13] Even so, it provides an interesting example of the way in which a justification of a kind of art can be based upon a severe division among the human faculties.

Proclus supposes three classes of poetry corresponding to three faculties in the human soul. The three faculties are arranged hierarchically and apparently function exclusively, not cooperatively. They include: a higher intuition capable of a kind of spiritual illumination; a form of discursive and analytic reasoning; and, lowest of all, the phantasy or imagination, which is irrational and responsive to appearances only. The matching forms of poetry are: the divinely inspired and mystical; the philosophical and didactic; and the imitative. This last type roughly echoes Plato's strictures on art in the *Republic*:

Sometimes it relies on a likeness alone, and sometimes it relies on a likeness that is only apparent, not real. It strongly intensifies very moderate passions, astonishing the hearers; using appropriate names and words, mutations of harmonies and varieties of rhythms, it changes the disposition of souls. It indicates the nature of things not as they are, but

as they appear to the many, being a certain adumbration,
and not an accurate knowledge of things. It also establishes
as its goal the delight of the hearers, and looks particularly
to the passive part of the soul, which is naturally adapted to
rejoice or be afflicted.[14]

This represents one way of interpreting Plato's views on
art and audience response. It involves a drastic rupture
of didactic and affective poetry, as well as the sacrifice of
its mimetic value, and it leads to theories that prize
poetry only when it is mystical or allegorical. However,
where Proclus seeks to part the didactic and affective,
based upon a psychology that appears to assign separate
kinds of function to the rational and intellective powers
of the soul on the one hand and the sensitive powers on
the other, later didactic theories sought earnestly to join
the two. And this reunion was in part premised on a
psychology that saw the various faculties working se-
quentially and in harmony.

Nor is the influence of Plato always in the direction
represented by Proclus, and we can notice three points
from which more positive results derived. First, there is
his acknowledgment in *Republic* VI that the mind can,
indeed must, use the imagery of the senses in a hypo-
thetical way. (Although for Plato such imagery is geo-
metrical or mathematical, that is perhaps less important
than the acknowledgment itself.) Second, he established,
albeit negatively, the tradition of associating the sensory
in art with affective response, and thus opened up the
question of its moral, social, and philosophical status.
Finally, his attention to problems of epistemology was,
through the agency of Plotinus and Augustine, rethought in medieval philosophy and in a context that
meant something for later theories of audience response.

AUGUSTINE

Augustine's massive effort to organize a Christian theology, as well as Plotinus's rethinking of Platonic dualism, are in most of their dimensions beyond the scope of this book, but we must notice, however, briefly, that their attention, and especially that of Augustine, to the processes of knowledge is significant for literary theory. Both tend to encourage the view that material images must be read allegorically and that this is a task for the rational intellect. Both follow Aristotle (and Plato) in describing knowledge as a kind of seeing, but their concepts of the orders of being and of what exists derive from Platonic dualism. They describe the mind doctrinally, not empirically, in order to demonstrate how the levels of being may be understood and valued. I shall give primary attention to the thought of Augustine.

His fundamental attitude towards the world is that it is instrumental and that our way of considering it should be conditioned by a desire to get beyond it, intellectually and spiritually. We should "use this world and not enjoy it" in an attempt to understand the "eternal and spiritual" by means of "corporal and temporal things."[15] At this point we can measure Augustine's position by reference to that of Plotinus, which is different. For Plotinus,

> Matter is not Soul; it is not Intellect; is not life, is no Ideal-Principle, no Reason-Principle; it is no limit or bound. . . . It will more plausibly be called a non-being . . . so that it is no more than the image and phantasm of Mass. . . . Its every utterance, therefore, is a lie; it pretends to be great and it is little, to be more and it is less; and the Existence with which it masks itself is no Existence, but a passing trick

making trickery of all that seems to be present in it, phantasms within a phantasm; it is like a mirror showing things as in itself when they are elsewhere, filled in appearance but actually empty, containing nothing, pretending everything. . . . Further: if visible objects were of the rank of the originals from which they have entered into matter we might believe Matter to be really affected by them, for we might credit them with some share in the power inherent in their senders: but the objects of our experiences are of very different virtue than the realities they represent, and we deduce that the seeming modification of matter by invisible things is unreal since the visible thing itself is unreal, having at no point any similarity with its source and cause.[16]

Augustine is far less drastic, insisting that sense perception, memory, and imagination may be accurate insofar as their proper spheres of knowledge are concerned. These in turn have a degree of reality. There are, he proposes, three general classes of things the mind can know: objects, representations of objects, and intellectual things. Allied to this there are three modes of vision: the corporeal, the spiritual (or imaginative), and the intellectual.[17] The latter requires no imaginative representation and is divided into two levels. The lower involves deliberative reasoning (*ratio inferior*), the higher a direct intuited knowledge, such as of God (*ratio superior*). Our concern here is with deliberative reason and with its relationship to imaginative activity, a relationship Augustine explores in some detail, primarily in *The Trinity*.

Like Aristotle, he describes knowing as stages proceeding from sense perception to abstract intellection, but instead of classifying sense perception as an animal or bodily function, he understands it as a case of the soul making use of the organs of the body. Therefore, although the external senses may register impressions, these do not become sensation (that is, they are not perceived) until images are recorded in the mind.[18] Augustine thus rejects, as Plotinus had, Aristotle's passive theory of perception, but unlike Plotinus he does not regard "lower" forms of perception as inevitable ignorance or confusion. Simple images are stored in the memory to be recovered at a later time. This recovery is intentional.[19] The intellect, in other words, is the substance that dominates and uses the body and its functions; all sentient or conscious life, even of the most elementary kind, is a function of mind, not body. Thus different modes of knowledge are not to be distinguished according to whether the faculties in play are faculties of body or of soul (in Aristotelian terms, of the sensitive or rational souls), but according to the kind of object the mind thinks about. Sight, memory, and imagination are bodily, rather than intellectual, potencies; but seeing, remembering, and imagining only take place when the mind decides to make use of these potencies.[20]

Memory allows the mind to contemplate the images of objects after the objects are no longer present to the sight, and memory is so closely related to the imagination as scarcely to differ from it. The image that remains in the memory Augustine calls a "phantasy." "Phantasm," on the other hand, is a term he reserves for something different: it is recovery by an act of will, not of a sense experience, but of an image constituted in the imagination from other remembered images. A phantasm is thus composite and in part invented, and the operation that produces it is akin to what was sometimes called "phantasy" in later medieval concepts of the soul.

For Augustine this process precedes knowledge.

His most extended discussion of imagination occurs in *The Trinity* in a context in which he seeks among other things to determine whether the imagination can be accurate and in which he considers problems of affect.[21] Remembering and imagining are voluntary acts and are a necessary prelude to actual thinking. Augustine is anxious to demonstrate that a proper knowledge of the natural and temporal world is neither mechanical nor reflexive, but instead a process in which the mind invokes immutable standards or ideas to inform and order its response to the material.[22] A pointed example shows how the intellect uses imagination:

> Thus, when I call to mind the walls of Carthage which I have seen, and form an image of those which I have not seen, and prefer some of these imaginary forms to others, I prefer them for a good reason; the judgment of the truth from above is strong and clear, and remains steadfast by the most incorruptible rules of its own right; and even if it is concealed by bodily images, as by a kind of cloud, still it is not hidden or confused.[23]

In the course of imagining an ideal is available to the mind, though not through the imagination alone, but also through the mind's access to some implanted universal standard: "Therefore," Augustine concludes, "we pass judgment on those particular things according to that form of the eternal truth, and we perceive that form through the eye of the rational mind."[24]

This attempt to suggest how the mind can move between universals and particulars and understand their relationship confines imagination to a strictly presentational role, and it may remind us of Aristotle's separation of imagination and opinion or judgment. But Augustine has a different motive. Any sense of truth the mind possesses "comes from above," and any attempt to invoke the paradigm is dependent upon a conjunction of imaginative presentation and the rational intellect. We have a process in which an idea is overlaid upon an image, though the image in some way derives from the idea (for the Platonic disposition behind Augustine's language is evident). In any case, this process of articulating or invoking a universal expressed in the imagination so that a particular may be judged or classified is described by Augustine as a kind of shedding of light in the mind. This is an aspect of his doctrine of illumination.

He next articulates a theory of communication:

> With the eye of the mind, therefore, we perceive in that eternal truth, from which all temporal things have been made, the form according to which we are, and by which we effect something either in ourselves or in bodies with a true and right reason. The true knowledge of things, thence conceived, we bear with us as a word, and beget by speaking from within; nor does it depart from us by being born. But in conversing with others we add the service of our voice or of some other bodily sign to the word that remains within, in order to produce in the mind of the listener, by a kind of sensible remembrance, something similar which does not depart from the mind of the speaker.[25]

Augustine is saying that there is a twofold relationship between idea and sign or material image. Sensible objects are indeed made after eternal truth; ideas are communicated through some kind of sensible sign.

Furthermore, understanding or illumination is a sort of actualization that takes place, much like turning on a light, when idea and image come together in the mind.

The possible application of these speculations to a theory of artistic making, and, more to the point of this study, to a theory of audience response, is beginning to emerge, but Augustine has not so far delivered himself of a concept of the mimetic or symbolic relationship between sensible and intelligible things. That any very evident connection is not to be had becomes clear when he suggests, in *De Genesi ad Litteram*, the qualitative difference between the viewing of an imaginative picture and a knowledgeable interpretation. There is, he says, in the spirit (that is, the imagination) "a certain power of the soul which is inferior to the mind, where likenesses of bodily things are expressed." His example is from the Old Testament: "And so Joseph was a greater prophet, who understood what the seven ears of corn and the seven kine meant, than Pharaoh, who saw them in a dream; for the spirit is informed by the thing so that it sees, the mind illuminated so that it understands."[26]

If the reason or intellect is the sole custodian of the significance of signs, the imagination nevertheless seems to have powers of affect. This appears to be the case when he notices truths expressed metaphorically:

> But why is it, I ask, that if anyone says this expresses divine truth abstractly, he delights his hearers less than if he had said the same thing in expounding that place in the Canticle of Canticles where it is said of the Church, as she is being praised as a beautiful woman, "Thy teeth are as flocks of sheep, that are shorn, which come up from the washing, all with twins and there is none barren among them"? Does one learn anything else besides that which he learns when

he hears the same thought expressed in plain words without this similitude? Nevertheless, in a strange way, I contemplate the saints more pleasantly when I envisage them as the teeth of the Church cutting off men from their errors and transferring them to her body after their hardness has been softened as if by being bitten and chewed.[27]

Imaginative presentation, though not necessary to comprehension, is more pleasing. And he seems to infer that no damage is done to the integrity of the idea. We should remember Augustine's view that the senses and imagination are brought to bear on objects by the direction of the will, which is an intellectual power. In such cases the will is also equivalent to desire. But the reverse may occur: ". . . these impressions of images are produced not only when the will is directed towards such things by desiring them, but also when the mind, in order to avoid them and to be on its guard against them, is impelled to look upon them so as to flee from them."[28] One difficulty in Augustine's theory is already apparent: having argued that even the most elementary sort of knowledge is voluntary and is an intellectual function that gives rise to images in the imagination, he now seems to imply that noticing objects may be happenstance. Only then can the mind's attention be concentrated to the extent that desire or aversion can result. Affect should, we might suppose, follow a degree of judgment as to whether an object is beneficial or harmful. We are thus confronted with a fairly substantial difference between Augustine's understanding of mental functions and the place of affect in them and that of Aristotle, whose concept of the soul's passive knowledge argues that affect may precede understanding.[29]

The point of interest for literary theory is this: what is

it in the image that attracts and affects the reader or
spectator? What is the source of his pleasure? Is it some
quality of the image which is capable eventually of
moving the will, or is pleasure produced because the
will, impelled by some condition within it, decides to
attend to an image? Augustine's account of the plastic
powers of the imagination would appear to suggest the
second alternative, if we are to judge by the following
passage:

> . . . because the mind possesses the great power of forming
> images, not only of things that it has forgotten, but also of
> those that it has not felt or experienced, while enlarging,
> diminishing, changing, or arranging at its pleasure those
> things which have not slipped away, it often fancies that
> something is so and so, when it knows either that it is not
> so, or does not know that it is so. In such a case it must
> take care that it does not either lie so as to deceive, or hold
> an opinion so as to be deceived. If it avoids these two faults,
> the phantasies of the imagination do not harm it, just as
> sensible things that have been experienced and retained in
> the memory do no harm if one does not desire them pas-
> sionately if they cause pleasure, or shamefully flee from
> them if they are unpleasant.[30]

That an image may "cause pleasure" or "be unplea-
sant" does not indicate some quality in the image as the
source of affect, but instead it is the mind's prior
possession of some idea or ideal pattern according to
which pleasure is produced as a consequence of voluntary attention. And when Augustine says "it fancies" or
"it knows," in each case he is designating the same
subject: these are operations of the mind in a certain
phase. We must keep in mind the distinction noticed

earlier between the imagination and imagining. Images
are presented in the imagination, but the active process
of imagining results from an intellectual decision. In this
sense the imagination is "creative," and the goodness or
badness of images is a result of the conjunction of their
presence in the mind and its disposition. In this context,
the following passage assumes that the mind's prior
possession of universal standards allows it to discover
and react to qualities in what it perceives:

> Certainly you love only the good, because the earth is good
> by the height of its mountains, the moderate elevation of its
> hills, and the evenness of its fields; and good is the farm that
> is pleasant and fertile; and good is the house that is arranged
> throughout in symmetrical proportions and is spacious and
> bright . . .; and good is the lecture that graciously instructs
> and suitably admonishes the listener; and good is the poem
> with its measured rhythm and the seriousness of its
> thoughts.[31]

The idea of the good, Augustine adds, has been "im-
pressed upon us,"[32] and it is by this aptitude that we are
able to value measure, balance, symmetry, and regularity
in nature and objects. Such kinds of esthetic judgment
are for Augustine paradigms of moral understanding as
well.

But the connections are not necessary or inevitable.
The divine ideas are independent of matter and not to be
directly approached by sensation.[33] Where Aristotle had
argued that the mind cannot think without images,
Augustine sees only an occasional connection between
truth and signs. Indeed his view of the operations of the
faculties which I have spent the past few pages reviewing is really what he calls "the trinity of the outer man,"

a mode of thinking which is at best practical reasoning and at worst a destructive addiction of the will to the world of sense. One kind of hierarchical and analogical connection between the phenomenal and noumenal seems missing in Augustine, in part because in his system the imagination is not a preliminary or lower form of thinking, but rather a power of presentation, which may combine images but does not abstract them.

The importance of imagination for a theory of audience response is directly outlined by Augustine in a letter to his friend Nebridius. Augustine says that there are three classes of mental images: accurate sense images, images of "things supposed," and images of thought. It is his account of the second class which concerns us:

> To the second class belong those images of things we imagine to have been so or to be so, as when for the sake of argument, we build up a certain case not repugnant to truth, or when we picture a situation to ourselves while a narrative is being read, or while we hear or compose or conjecture some fabulous tale. When it pleases me or when it comes to my mind, I can picture to myself the appearance of Aeneas, or of Medea with winged serpents yoked to her chariot, or of Chremes or of some Parmeno. Of this class, also, are those images which the learned make use of as figures to illustrate truth, and those which the ignorant, founders of various superstitions, allege as true: for example the infernal Phlegethon, and the five caverns of the inhabitants of the dark regions, and the northern stake supporting the sky, and a thousand other portents of poets and heretics. Thus we say, in the course of an argument: imagine three worlds like this one, piled one on top of the other; imagine the earth confined in a square figure, and such things. For we imagine and suppose all these things according to the tenor of our thought.[34]

The mental process of the poet is precisely the same as that of the reader: for both the picture and the idea it illustrates involve a deliberate, willed mental action, a making of a fiction that may or may not accord with true doctrine but nevertheless is intellectually useful so long as it is not taken literally. We must not, Augustine implies, "allege as true" that which is merely exemplary.

AQUINAS

Scholastic psychology in its main features amounts to a commentary upon the observations of Aristotle, and it is closely related to a concept of thinking in which the mind moves from the observation of particular, material sensations to the universals that may be abstracted from them. This way of construing the relationship between the universal and the particular is quite different from that of Augustine. Augustine argues that the idea is prior to the particular and determines the way in which the particular should be understood: the image of the particular in the mind is a means of illustrating and communicating universals the mind already possesses. From an Augustinian point of view particular images make universal truths more concrete, vivid, and easy to articulate. The Scholastic view is that the contemplation of particulars is the beginning of our understanding of universals. The universal is a condition by which a particular object belongs to a class of objects, and this means that particular images, including the images of fictional art, have a kind of reality as members of a class of objects which Platonic and Neoplatonic philosophy would deny. For Augustine the phantasm or image that the imagination derives from memory or sensation is a

presentation only. No universal inheres in it, for universals exist only in the mind of God. For Aquinas the
universal is incarnate in the particular object and hence
in its image. The Scholastic qualification is that reality,
which is both material and immaterial, is arranged in
such a way that all created being is a continuous, related
hierarchy. In the human mind this hierarchy determines
the relationship of body and mind, the union of which
establishes our vital existence in a servant-master relationship and on a broader scale places man at the bottom
of the order of intellectual creatures. Therefore it is the
quality of his mental power which limits man's ability to
know the most abstruse and eternal truths, not the
defects of material and particular objects. In the Scholastic view man is capable of knowing sensible objects in
their species and essence.[35] This capacity Aquinas calls
"an abstractive power of understanding" (*S.T.* Ia. 79.
3),[36] and it is joined with the perceptive powers of the
mind so that the passive powers of the sensitive soul
responding to matter are the beginning of the process of
knowledge.

Aquinas adopts the Aristotelian view that the soul
must think about matter through the images or species
as they appear in the inner senses, and his concept of the
imagination is thus strictly Aristotelian. Imagination is a
power of retaining sense forms: "So for the reception of
sense forms there is the particular sense and the 'common' sense . . . Their retention and conservation require fantasy or imagination, which are the same thing;
fantasy or imagination is, as it were, a treasure-store of
forms received through the senses." Also the mind has
the power of cogitation, which in animals is called
"instinct" and which fastens upon "intentions" (whether

something is to be avoided or welcomed). The imagination is a single power that has two basic functions, to reproduce the images of objects and to combine disparate images into new wholes.[37]

As with Aristotle, the imagination for Aquinas is essential to any kind of knowledge: ". . . for the intellect actually to understand (not only in acquiring new knowledge but also in using knowledge already acquired), acts of the imagination and other faculties are required" (*S.T.* Ia. 84. 7). Furthermore, images are both copies of things that have a reality and are exemplary: they are necessary both for comprehension and explanation. This dependence originates in the fact that

> corporeal reality, has as its proper object intelligible substances separate from corporeal reality, and it is by means of these intelligible objects that it knows material realities. The proper object of the human intellect, on the other hand, since it is joined to a body, is a nature of "whatness" found in corporeal matter—*the intellect, in fact, rises to the limited knowledge it has of invisible things by way of the nature of visible things* [italics added]. . . . Now we apprehend the particular through the senses and the imagination. Therefore if it is actually to understand its proper subject, then the intellect must needs turn to sense images in order to look at universal natures existing in particular things. (*S.T.* Ia. 84. 8)

This passage underscores the crucial differences in the epistemologies of Augustine and Aquinas. Augustine would not agree that sensible or material particulars possess a "reality" or embody universals; nor would he concede that they are the proper "subjects" of human understanding. It is not entirely facetious to suggest that

Augustine's view of the human intellect is close to that which Aquinas assigns to angels: certainly it is the task of the human intellect as Augustine construes it to aspire to a mode of contemplation which uses imagery only in a provisional way, to communicate and explain by means of something that has no necessary relation to idea or universal.[38]

Since we are concerned with the significance of these matters in didactic theory, we can infer that the Scholastic view of the imagination and its role in perception and thought suits very well a concept of literature in which the imagery is both mimetic and exemplary and can be so understood by the audience. The system of Augustine is, in theory at least, more appropriate to works that employ the veil of allegory and in which the imagery is arbitrary and convenient at best. In other terms we can express the difference by repeating Augustine's belief that the perspicuity of the interpreting mind lends significance to the image: "And so Joseph was a greater prophet, who understood what the seven kine and the seven ears of corn meant, than Pharaoh, who saw them in a dream; for the spirit (i.e. the imagination) is informed by the things so that it sees, the mind illuminated so that it understands."[39]

Aquinas's views of the connections between knowledge and appetite begins in a negative argument concerning the ability of imagination to move the soul. In his commentary on *De Anima*, he mentions that in the absence of rational guidance the imagination may prompt attraction or withdrawal from a perceived object or image. This may happen when the intellect is veiled, either by some passion, by insanity, or in dreams.[40] We

meet here the usual hesitations about imaginative experience which run through the entire history of faculty
psychology. But there is also a way of establishing
positive connections between intellect, imagination, and
will. For Aquinas, as for Aristotle, the cogitative power
decides the affective status of a perceived object. Perception thus involves a preliminary or rudimentary judgment before the "agent intellect" classifies it (*S.T.* Ia. 78.
4). Not all perception produces an affective response,
but such a response is not possible unless preliminary
judgment occurs. Both derive from the value judgment
made on the basis of perception, but different levels of
desire or aversion result from different levels of knowledge, even though the intellectual appetite may be
turned to a concrete particular. "Intellectual appetite,
though it bears on objects which exist outside the soul as
concrete particulars, nevertheless attains in them a universal object of reason, desiring a thing because it is
good. Thus Aristotle observes in his *Rhetoric* that hate can
bear on something universal, as when *we hate every type
of thief*."[41]

Here we have a strong clue to the way in which
images of particular things in a literary context can have
both the status of universals and produce, albeit in a
very rough and obvious way, an emotional response.
Moreover, Aquinas recognizes that the basic appetites,
which he calls "desirousness" and "aggressiveness"
(the concupiscible and irascible appetites) have complex
relationships to reason, will, imagination, and sensation. They may be directed by the higher, rational
powers or conflict with them: "We experience conflict
between reason on the one hand and aggression and

desire on the other when we sense or imagine a pleasure reason forbids or feel sad at something reason commands" (*S.T.* Ia. 81. 3). Even in the absence of an external object, imagined objects of desire can excite or modify the appetite.[42] The imagination can make up things, and this formative process was sometimes held to be a creative form of thinking. As Murray Bundy has recorded, there is a line of thought in late classical and medieval psychological theory which gives some weight to the inventive properties of imagination.[43]

For our purposes what is important to note is how closely medieval psychology linked the functions of appetite and internal picturing. Appetite was considered ubiquitous and nearly inevitable, an irreducible basic response of desire or aversion whenever the attention was drawn to something within the mind or without. A corollary proposition is that the mind is apt to believe that whatever is initially attractive is morally good. Plato had recognized the trap in this disposition and argued that only accurate knowledge would permit us to find goodness attractive and evil repellent. One line of late medieval and Renaissance thought worked in this direction, emphasizing the supremacy of the contemplative life and encouraging a poetic devoted to the objective of ultimate truth. But the disposition of didactic theory was to argue that the responsibility of the poet was to create morally valid images to prevent the misdirection of the reader's imagination and will. Most philosophers, especially those interested in faculty psychology, acknowledged the ambiguity of imagining, a process that, without strong ethical and rational direction, could produce vivid and destructive illusions. The poet's task was to present fictions at once vital, stimulating, and properly related to truth, appealing first of all to the very faculty and its attendant appetites which were, if left to chance, the source of error.

SUMMARY

In the concepts of mental activity we have reviewed there are two different motives at work. One, which finds its origins in Platonic idealism, believes that the chief aim of thinking is to approach unchanging, disembodied truth and to use the mind's possession of it when in contact with the particulars of the natural and human world. This means that the images carried in the imagination may be used, but not believed in. If they are believed in or granted some kind of substantiality, they become a screen between the mind and its awareness of the truth, and the affective power of the imagination, especially where, as in literature or art, images of objects may seem credible and real, is dangerous. The other motive, which stems from Aristotle, does allow a measure of validity to particular objects or actions, and hence to their images. Furthermore, in insisting that all thinking must begin in the perception of images, Aristotelian and Scholastic epistemology eventually helped to encourage theories of literature which sought to place reliance on the very faculties—sense and imagination, and through them, the passions and appetites—which Neoplatonism in its several forms tended to disparage. Once again, it must be said that both traditions of thought used a general psychology whose origins are in Aristotle's *De Anima*, even though this psychology might be employed in the service of rather different and various philosophical systems.

Aristotelian psychology continued to dominate in the Renaissance, where the record of comment on the nature of the soul is extensive.[44] It includes such diverse interests as the immortality of the soul, the freedom of the will, the nature of love, ethics, physiology and medicine, and the study of temperament. Philosophical positions range from Neoplatonism, Augustinianism, and Stoicism to more or less orthodox Scholasticism, but Renaissance thinkers are notorious for borrowing liberally what they wanted from a variety of classical and medieval sources, for blurring older distinctions between philosophical systems, and for attempting syntheses where there had once been sharp divisions. The history of faculty psychology shows the Aristotelian tradition cutting across both older diversities and newer combinations to survive largely intact through the sixteenth century and beyond. Typical of the resort to Aristotle for an account of the basic processes of feeling and thought is a treatise on the imagination by Gianfrancesco Pico Della Mirandola. The work is saturated with distrust of the imagination and crammed with hints for avoiding the consequences of its delusive assaults on reason. Yet Pico accepts the Aristotelian description of the imagination and other faculties and concedes that we must have it to function as living beings.[45] Neoplatonic philosophy generally tended to echo this acceptance and to combine faculty psychology with a version of Augustine's belief that sentient and imaginative experience amount to the use of the lower faculties by the rational intellect.[46] Neo-Stoics such as Vives shared this view, emphasizing the power of rational will to dampen appetite through the use of the imagination.[47] It would indeed be strange if didactic theorists had avoided common ground, and in fact those critics most attentive to the nature of the audience accepted established psychological doctrine. But, unlike such figures as Ficino or Bruno, they did not do so in order to reinforce a belief in the value of contemplation. They were a good bit more worldly in the best sense of the word.

The direction I am suggesting may be illustrated in the attitudes of Coluccio Salutati, who sought to establish an intellectual structure of traditional theology and philosophy based on Augustinian theology and pointed at the reformation of the will.[48] At the same time his epistemology is Aristotelian and Scholastic, and so is his psychology: following Aristotle and Aquinas he believed that the mind moves analogically from image to concept. Knowledge occurs when perception passes from the senses to the common sense to imagination, and thence to judgment, memory, and intellect, which presents both images and concepts to the will.[49] When he comes to discuss the impact of poetry Salutati argues that the reader's imagination can be touched directly and moved delightfully by elements of style at the same time as the intellect is able to perceive a covert meaning:

And I conceive imaginary discourse to be that which by saying one thing and meaning something else moves the imagination and even the phantasy. Because the part assigned to description touches certain discourses more openly, while truth is hidden under the mystery of some narration which is occult. For it is peculiar to the poet in metric and figurative speech to move the imaginative faculty in such a way that our intellect sees the words themselves by a certain similitude and perceives what is said and understands something other than what is narrated.[50]

For Salutati the pleasing surface of imaginative discourse is buttressed and validated by the hidden meaning. We are not yet in the presence of a theory in which
the mimetic quality of imagery is simultaneously delightful and instructive. But it is not far off. Poetry is of
supreme consequence in a system where knowledge
must be directed to moral choice because poetry supplies
the mode of language by which the mind moves from
the seen to the unseen: "It is clear that not only when we
speak of God but also when we talk about incorporeal
beings we speak of them improperly and according to
the outer shell and what we say is false. . . . Poetry
should therefore be defined as that mode of speaking
which understands both things and words as something
other than it shows them."[51] But this process still
involves a kind of analogy: poetic speech, he believes,
conveys a meaning "other than what it shows, moving
the phantasy by similitude and touching both the sense
and informing the intellect at the same time."[52] Finally,
Salutati acknowledges a kind of temporary belief on the
part of the reader in the imagined beauty or ugliness
created by poets, suggesting that this sort of response
is natural and cannot reasonably be forbidden to
Christians.[53]

This represents an important point in the general
context of Renaissance didactic theory and that of Dante
as well, for it places poetic language and fable, and the
reader's imaginative powers, at the center of two mental
processes, one moving from sense impression to concept
and the other involving the image in the movement of
the will. If we subtract Dante's belief in divine inspiration, we have in Salutati precisely the kinds of focus and
affective process Dante acts out in the *Purgatorio*: the

image acting on the imagination compels delight; the reason acting on the image receives truth; together they generate the intellectual appetite—the will—and move the soul toward virtue. Salutati's goal is the reform of the will in this life; Dante looks more directly to the afterlife and salvation, but both reconcile the features of Augustinian and Aristotelian epistemology which we have examined in this chapter. Both propose that poetry and art should use the imagery of sensory experience instrumentally; yet both also acknowledge a kind of analogical status to particulars. As we shall see in the next chapter, this compromise, together with a belief in the power of imagination, allows Dante to assign an important territory to art in the process of moral education.

II

Dante's Esthetic of Grace and the Reader's Imagination

At the close of the preceding chapter we noted in the example of the fifteenth-century Humanist Coluccio Salutati an attempt to combine Augustine's theology of the will and his concept of the "instrumental" use of fictional images with a psychology that is Aristotelian and Scholastic in origin. Salutati was not the first to propose such a combination. It appears at least a century earlier in some of the writings of Dante, most notably and completely in the *Purgatorio*. Dante's theology and the more intricate details of his allegory are in most respects well outside the scope of this study, but one point of focus is central and determinate, both for his presentation of the soul's journey to salvation and for his view of the role of poetry and art in this process. This point is his interest in the education and conversion of the will, and we must keep it steadily in mind as we

examine what he has to say about the artistic image and
the faculties of the audience.

Early in *De Vulgari Eloquentia* (ca. 1304) Dante remarks
on the necessity that "the human race have some sign, at
once rational and sensible, for the intercommunication
of its thoughts."[1] The "sign," which is language, arises
from the mixed nature of the human soul, both passionate and rational but unable in mortal existence to be
wholly one or the other. Human beings, therefore,
cannot know one another as animals do through silent
and instant communication but must make do with the
imagery of the senses rationally construed. But if man is
inevitably bound to his vegetative and sensible nature,
he is nevertheless distinguished by his "angelic" or
rational gifts, and because of these, as Dante says in the
Convivio, he "has an affinity for truth and virtue."[2] This
affinity is natural and tends to draw the human soul
beyond the material: "And the soul of man which is
endowed with the nobility of the highest faculty, namely, reason, participates in the divine nature under the
aspect of everlasting intelligence. For the soul in this
supreme faculty is so much ennobled and so completely
divested of matter that the divine light streams into it as
into an angel, and hence man is called by philosophers a
divine animal."[3]

Such participation in the divine is at best a potential
capacity of mind, for mortal man is in a state of becom-
ing and suffers from an imperfect capacity to communicate. The mind is sometimes able to perceive the super-
sensible truths which Dante calls "ineffable," but this
power is dim and imperfect.

I say that our intellect for lack of that virtue by which it
draws to itself that which it perceives (I mean an organic

virtue, namely, imagination), cannot rise to certain things because the imagination cannot help it, as it has not the wherewithal. Such, for example, are substances separate from matter, which, although we may to some extent speculate about them, we cannot understand or apprehend perfectly. . . . Furthermore, a limit is set to our ability in all its operations not by ourselves but by universal nature, and therefore we must know that the bounds of our capacity give wider range for thought than for speech, and wider range for speech than for the language of signs.[4]

Dante's view of the human mind not only proposes its limitations but also presents it struggling against them. The immaterialities we fail to understand perfectly are nevertheless urgent, so that even as he accepts the divinely established imperfections of the imagination, his poetry constantly exhibits the temperament of one who would know more and who would furthermore realize that knowledge in the most concrete terms. Yet what he wishes to know and to convey stretches beyond nature, even as it never ceases to include it, and he thus requires some theory of knowledge and a psychology that permits universals to be expressed in images if he is to remain a poet. Dante's struggle, on one level, is that of the poet seeking an epistemology and a rhetoric that will testify simultaneously to the natural handicaps of the artist and the utter necessity of working against them for his own rescue and that of his readers. One of his solutions is to be found in his self-consciousness as a poet: he sometimes seems the most self-absorbed of all medieval artists, making his own sensibility the center of all his imaginative work from the *Vita Nuova* to the *Commedia*. Playing the dual role of poet and protagonist, at moments which are crucial for this discussion, he becomes, for all practical purposes, the reader and spectator as well.

The *Commedia*, where these various roles are most completely folded into the fictional whole, is supremely a narrative of epistemological quest. From beginning to end the protagonist is driven by a thirst to know and to understand, to force his soul to as much ultimate knowledge with as much clarity and conviction as he is able, and as God may provide, and once we become aware of how drastically Dante, as a figure in the poem, is absorbed in the search, it is a temptation to regard the nature and purpose of the poem as a mystic vision to the detriment of other features.[5] However, there is a corrective in the letter to Can Grande, where Dante asserts that "the branch of philosophy which regulates the work in its whole and in its parts, is morals or ethics, because the whole was undertaken not for speculation but for practical results." These results are didactic and persuasive: "to remove those living in this life from the state of misery and lead them to the state of felicity."[6] Dante's purpose as artist reminds us that the *Inferno* and *Purgatorio* should not be slighted for the sake of the *Paradiso* and, by inference, that Dante's interest in the conditions of mortal existence is as fully realized as his vision of salvation. If we consider the whole, as he insists that we do, we may avoid the inclination to construe its purpose as totally visionary and seek to respond to an esthetic aimed at moral education as well as at spiritual enlightenment. To understand this esthetic we need to measure Dante's attention to psychology.

The earliest evidence of a concern for the processes of affect appears in the *Vita Nuova* in a context that establishes powerful bonds between modes of feeling and imagination on the one hand and the artistic image on the other. The *Vita Nuova* is an account of idealized, obsessive, internalized desire. Its action is inward, and although the verse and Dante's explanatory comments in prose are highly organized and rationalized, his effort is also to convey the most powerful and concentrated feeling. So much is evident from the beginning. "When there appeared before my eyes the now glorious lady of my mind," Dante begins, the " 'vital spirit' began to tremble violently."[7] There follows a detailed rendering of the effects of desire in terms of physiological psychology. The "animal spirit" was amazed and perceived its bliss. The "natural spirit," located in the stomach, began to weep, sensing the loss of freedom. So precise an account of affect in the heart, head, and stomach according to the medical conventions of the time seeks to convey the manner in which physical sensation and perception are translated into passion.[8] Physical affect is matched by the perturbation of the soul and by mental impression, and these endure in the poet's memory and imagination. Indeed Dante calls the *Vita Nuova* his "book of memory."[9]

> Let me say that, from that time on, Love governed my soul, which become immediately devoted to him, and he reigned over me with such assurance and lordship, given him by the power of my imagination, that I could only dedicate myself to fulfilling his every pleasure. (Chapter 2)

Subsequently the poet's imagination and memory continue to recover the image of Beatrice: they are the faculties that keep the object of desire present in the mind and vital to the affections. They are also the occasion of dreams and daydreams (Chapters 3, 9, 12, 23, 24, 34, and 42). These may be either erroneous or prophetic; they prompt the poet to write verse and to comment on his emotional and physical condition; and above all they reveal the imagination moving beyond the simple recovery of the image of Beatrice to the creation of narrative situations. Although the act of composing poems seems to be voluntary, the mental and emotional states these poems express are not. From the outset Dante is love's prisoner: " 'If I did not lose my wits and felt able to answer her, I would tell her that as soon as I call to mind the miraculous image of her beauty, then the desire to see her overcomes me, a desire so powerful that it kills, it destroys anything in my memory that might have been able to restrain it' " (Chapter 15). Desire and imagination work reciprocally on one another, but sight, the image of Beatrice, and hence the quickened imagination are the sources of his preoccupation and from time to time the immediate occasion for poetic composition.

In Chapter 3 the first of the dreams suggests to us that the imagery of such experience is like that of a work of art. Dante has just seen Beatrice for the second time, nine years after the first encounter:

and passing along a certain street, she turned her eyes to where I was standing faint-hearted and, with that indescribable graciousness for which today she is rewarded in the eternal life, she greeted me so miraculously that I seemed at that moment to behold the entire range of possible bliss. It was precisely the ninth hour of that day, three o'clock in the afternoon, when her sweet greeting came to me. Since this

was the first time her words had ever been directed to me,
I became so ecstatic that, like a drunken man, I turned away
from everyone and I sought the loneliness of my room,
where I began thinking of this most gracious lady and,
thinking of her, I fell into a sweet sleep, and a marvelous
vision appeared to me.

In this vision Love appears carrying Beatrice, lightly
clothed in red, in his arms. He gives her a fiery object,
the dreamer's heart, and makes her eat it. To the
dreamer's anguish they abruptly depart towards the
heavens, and his sleep is broken. Dante then decides to
write a poem "addressed to all Love's faithful subjects;
and requesting them to interpret my vision, I would
write them what I had seen in my sleep." The poem, "A
ciascun'alma presa e gentil core," recounts the dream in
somewhat briefer form than the prose narrative. There is
no indication that the source of the vision is outside the
poet's mind or that it has been generated by anything
other than Beatrice's greeting. The quality of imagination encountered here is nevertheless literary and al-
legorial, a poet's dream; yet as lover Dante is acted upon
and remains passive. The poem he writes is a record of
what he has dreamt, so that we are left with the
impression that he is essentially a spectator, though one
whose feelings are deeply engaged.[10]

With the exception of Dante's final "miraculous"
vision in Chapter 42, an event referred to but not described, the dreams tend, like that in Chapter 3, to result
from concentrated thought or meditation and thus appear as an extension of the lover's condition. Either they
help to clarify his mind, as in Chapters 9 and 12, or they
exhibit some prophetic element. The content of most of
them is highly emotional; we are meant, I think, to
understand these visions as moments of crisis. All but

the last two are dramatic as well as pictorial: the dreamer is involved in dialogue and in some interaction with other figures, usually the god of love. The fictional mode of the dreams varies from the allegorical to the realistic. The dreams have sometimes been interpreted as record- ing the destructive power of the imagination, the ten- dency of the sensitive soul in the grip of passion to lead the mind into erroneous judgment, but such readings tend to reduce the imaginative experiences in the *Vita Nuova* to psychological case studies.[11] The issue is more complex.

In the first place imagination emerges from the dreams and visions of the *Vita Nuova* as a clarifying power. The clarification is not always welcome: at one point Dante remarks (Chapter 16), " . . . many times I suffered when my memory excited my imagination to re-evoke the transformations that Love worked in me." The power of imagination helps make him the creature of love, but it also, in the first dream, presents this situation in icono- graphic terms that provide him with a greater under- standing of his predicament and prompt the first lyric. The dream in Chapter 9, in which Love appears as "a pilgrim scantily and poorly dressed," occasions another poem and gives him the idea of pretending to fix his emotions on another woman than Beatrice as a "de- fense." In Chapter 12 Love appears to him to explain why Beatrice has avoided him and to suggest how he may assure that she will "set the proper value on the words of those people who are mistaken." Even the powerful and deluded vision of Chapter 23, in which Dante sees women who tell him, "You are going to die," and who announce the death of Beatrice, is ultimately prophetic, though as a vivid account of the immediate present it is full of wild illusions and vain imaginings.

One of the more crucial dreams follows in Chapter 24. Here Love appears for the last time and announces, "Anyone of subtle discernment would call Beatrice Love, because she so greatly resembles me."[12]

In Chapter 25 Dante explains at some length the kind of art he practices. The god of love who has been appearing in his visions is an invention, the device of personification inherited from the Latin poets.

> At this point it may be that someone worthy of having every doubt cleared up could be puzzled at my speaking of Love as if it were a thing in itself, as if it were not only an intellectual substance, but also a bodily substance. This is patently false, for Love does not exist in itself as a substance, but is an accident in a substance. And that I speak of Love as if it possessed a body, further still, as if it were a human being, is shown by three things I say about it. I say that I saw it coming; and since "to come" implies locomotion, and since, according to the Philosopher, only a body may move from place to place by its own power, it is obvious that I assume Love to be a body. I also say that it laughed and even that it spoke—acts that would seem characteristic of a human being, especially that of laughing; and so it is clear that I assume love to be human.

After tracing this version of poetic license from the Latin poets to its use in the vernacular, Dante repeats his account of personification in terms conventionally used to describe the process of imagination:

> So, if we find that the Latin poets addressed inanimate objects in their writings, as if these objects had sense and reason, or address each other, and that they did this not only with real things but also with unreal things (that is: they have said, concerning things that do not exist, that they

speak, and they have said that many an accident in substance speaks as if it were a substance and human), then it is
fitting that the vernacular poet do the same—not, of course,
without some reason, but with a motive that later can be
explained in prose.

In thus explaining some of the motives and devices of
his art, Dante is suggesting that thought and feeling are
linked in the mind of the lover with imagination and that
the poet must realize and present these activities in
human images: in bringing them to a state of embodied
personification he prepares the way for a rational understanding of their significance.

The imagination as an inventive faculty has a limited
role in the *Vita Nuova*, amounting to the fashioning of
images that may be translated into prose and thus
rationalized. Dealing with accidents, it confines itself to
externals such as sight, sound, color, shape, arrangement of images, and the like, qualities quite distinct from
the essence of things. But in the phantasy of the dreamer
or spectator these images renew and perpetuate feeling,
often to the point of concentrated violence. If we consider these images strictly from the standpoint of the
individual who experiences them in his imagination,
they are indeed little more than the occasion for or
expression of disturbing emotions whose direction and
significance he has difficulty in understanding. This is
not to say that the *Vita Nuova* resists interpretation, but
rather that we cannot look for that interpretation in the
reactions of the protagonist, or at least we find some clue
to it only to the extent that the experience of his imagination progressively goads him toward a partial understanding. There are hints of progress in Chapter 39,
where a briefly narrated vision suggests Beatrice in glory

and causes him to repent his attentions to other women, and further hints occur in the concluding chapter. He has begun to look upon these visions as the threshold to higher forms of thought.

The relationship between images in the mind and their rational analysis is taken up in *Convivio*, III, ii, where Dante borrows a description of the powers of the intellect—"this noblest part of the soul"—from Aristotle: "there is in it one ability which is called scientific, and another which is called ratiocinative or deliberative, and attendant upon these are certain other abilities, as Aristotle affirms in that same passage, as, for example, those of imagination and judgment."[13] Dante's term is *inventiva*, a rendering of Aristotle's "deliberative imagination" (*De Anima*, 434a), which involves a form of thinking close to and supportive of reasoning. The daydream in *Vita Nuova*, Chapter 39, recounts a comparable interplay between imaginative vision, reason, and the direction of the will.

> One day, about the ninth hour, there arose in me against this adversary of reason a powerful vision, in which I seemed to see that glorious Beatrice clothed in those crimson garments with which she first appeared to my eyes, and she seemed young, of the same age as when I first saw her. Then I began to think about her and, remembering her in the sequence of past times, my heart began to repent painfully of the desire by which it so basely let itself be possessed for some time, contrary to the constancy of reason; and once I had discarded this evil desire, all my thoughts turned back to their most gracious Beatrice.

Here Dante's imagination and memory have properly supported a reasoned decision. The recollected image of Beatrice is far from a casual detail, for it is what allows him to choose one object of affection over another. Within his own mind he is the viewer of the product of his own faculties and finally responsive to what they show him.

In Chapter 42 he mentions his last vision, this time "miraculous," and resolves to write no more about Beatrice until he is capable of doing so in a "nobler" way. His admission of the incompleteness of the *Vita Nuova* seems partly a sense of insufficient insight and partly an expression of the desire of the will to come to terms with its own destiny. This involves the mind's use and understanding of what it sees and knows; in other terms it is the problem of how to respond to perceptions of the material world. The mind, because it is linked with the body and sees through the agency of the body, can think only in terms of material and sensible images, and this assumption clarifies Dante's reference in *De Vulgari Eloquentia* to the natural weakness of the human intellect and accounts in a broad sense for the double status of images as reflections of the material world on the one hand and as signs on the other.

These propositions inform the *Commedia*, and in the *Purgatorio* especially they give point to the didactic process at the center of that stage of Dante's journey. The *Purgatorio*, if we attend to the allegory, deals with the substance of doctrine to be learned in this life, but it also draws our attention to the ways in which doctrine enters the mind. Once again Dante is poet, protagonist, and spectator, and by paying special attention to Dante as protagonist and spectator, we will discover something of his attitudes towards art.

The *Purgatorio* is shaped by the motive of the reformation of the will, a reformation necessary to prepare the soul for paradise and therefore bound up inseparably with the soul's quest for knowledge. There is for Dante no such thing as disinterested knowing; knowledge in one way or another is a function of love, and love, as Marco Lombardo explains in Canto XVI, implies free will:

> ". . . a light is given you to know good and evil, and free will, which if it endure fatigue in its first battles with the heavens, afterwards, if it is well nurtured, it conquers completely. You lie subject, in your freedom, to a greater power and to a better nature, and that creates the mind in you which the heavens have not in their charge. . . ." (16. 75—81)

But the use of this power must be learned, for at the outset our natural inclination is impulsive: " ' . . . the simple little soul, which knows nothing, save that, proceeding from a glad Maker, it turns eagerly to what delights it. First it tastes the savor of a trifling good: there it is beguiled and runs after it, if guide or curb bend not its love' " (16. 88—93).[14] These passages prepare for the lectures in Cantos 17 and 18 in which Virgil explains the human appetite, both natural and intellectual. First:

> "Neither Creator nor creature, my son, was ever without love, either natural or of the mind, and this you know. The natural is always without error; but the other may err either through too much or too little vigor. While it is directed on the Primal Good, and on secondary goods observes right measure, it cannot be the cause of sinful pleasure. But when it is turned awry to evil, or speeds to good with more zeal, or with less, than it ought, against the Creator works His creature. Hence you can comprehend that love must needs be the seed in you of every virtue and of every action deserving punishment." (17. 91—105)

How, then, can appetite be controlled? Virgil's answer is elaborate:

> "The mind, which is created quick to love, is responsive to everything that pleases, as soon as by pleasure it is roused to action. Your faculty of apprehension draws an image from a real existence and displays it within you, so that it makes the mind turn to it; and if, thus turned, the mind inclines toward it, that inclination is love, that inclination is nature which is bound in you anew by pleasure. Then, even as the fire moves upward by reason of its form, being born to ascend thither where it lasts longest in its matter, so the captive mind enters into desire, which is a spiritual movement, and never rests until the thing loved makes it rejoice. Now it may be apparent to you how far the truth is hidden from people who aver that every love is praiseworthy in itself, because perhaps its matter appears to be good: but not every imprint is good, although the wax be good." (18. 19–39)

What Virgil is suggesting is that if the mind mistakes the image within it for the object itself, it may be led astray. We have, he continues, a "specific virtue" that we can only deduce by its effects. In itself this virtue is morally neutral; it is a basic aptitude for judgment and choice. Praise or blame must therefore be assigned to the quality of specific judgments and choices, according as they are directed to proper or improper objects. Thus human freedom lies not in the power to choose or not to choose, but in the capacity for correct or incorrect decisions. Once a decision has been made, the dynamics of feeling are self-propelled (11. 49–66). What Virgil does not or cannot explain is how the judgment and will can be trained. He has located those powers of the soul which function by necessity and isolated the boundaries of choice, but it is left to the action of the *Purgatorio*, and, as Virgil concludes, to Beatrice, to illuminate the process of education.

The means of this education is a kind of art, an ordered and designed context through which Dante moves, and which in part precedes the expositions of Marco and Virgil. There is first of all a careful and pointed distinction made in the *Purgatorio* between experience of the world of nature and the experience of art. There is also in Canto 2 a glance backward to a kind of art no longer useful, though still sweet and poignant to recall. Dante comes upon the musician Casella and asks him to sing one of his early lyrics, "Amor che ne la mente mi ragiona" ("Love that discourses in my mind"). Casella sings "so sweetly that the sweetness still within me sounds" (11. 113–114). For a moment the listeners are held "content as if naught else touched the mind of any" (11. 116–117), but Cato roughly breaks in and beckons them towards a "greater care." This moment in which the attention is turned away from earthly preoccupation anticipates the transition from Antepurgatory to the purgatorial terraces, from the natural loveliness of the Valley of the Princes to the gates at the entrance to Purgatory proper. It is also a transition from the surroundings of more or less natural imagery to that furnished by religious art.

The difference in the orders of image with which Dante's mind has to contend becomes apparent as he approaches the end of Antepurgatory. There are two sources of imagery: the immediate material environment of terrain, sights, sounds, and the figures he encounters; and the pilgrim's mental environment revealed in his dreams and in what he tells us he thought. Both kinds of imagery are colored by Dante's way of presenting them.

In the external realm appearances are largely "natural-istic." The landscape is not grotesque (especially in contrast to that of the *Inferno*), and the figures he meets seem more or less as they might have been in mortal life. The first change occurs in Canto 8, where Dante and Virgil witness the pageant of the green-winged angels and the serpent; divine iconography begins to dominate the scene.

The sensory quality of the Mount of Purgatory con-trasts sharply with the naturalism of Antepurgatory. As the narrative moves towards the mountain, Dante re-minds us of a church bell tolling compline. This is followed by a hymn, "Te lucis ante," and the pageant of the angels and the serpent. In Canto 9, Dante falls asleep and dreams that he is being carried aloft by an eagle symbolizing divine grace; when he wakes he discovers that St. Lucy has carried him up the initially precipitous approach to the gate. Before the gate are three different-ly colored steps and an angel dressed in ecclesiastical robes standing guard. He announces that he holds the keys "from Peter." The canto ends with religious music: "I turned attentive to the first note and *'Te Deum laudamus'* I seemed to hear in a voice mingled with sweet music. What I heard gave me the same impression we sometimes get when people are singing with an organ, and now the words are clear and now are not" (11. 139–145). The intaglio carvings in Canto 10, more prayers and hymns, and the carvings on the floor in Canto 12 suggest that the purgatorial environment is indeed churchly, that Dante, Virgil, and the souls being pun-ished on each level are being systematically exposed to the sacramental and doctrinal experience of the true Church.

Added to the reminders of ecclesiastical surroundings

is an insistence on the artful quality of the place. In Canto 9 Dante, asking the reader not to wonder if he sustains his theme with greater art, seeks to match his efforts to the art of God. Two Renaissance editors, Landino and Vellutello, interpret this request to mean that the poet is self-consciously shifting to a more elevated style, which includes a greater use of figure and metaphor, as well as a more formal rhetorical rhythm.[15] Of course, more than language is involved: everything described conveys order, harmony, balance, and de-liberation. There is, apparently, no random or "natural" way to the reformation of the will. Art is presented both as part of the physical surroundings and as the imagery of dreams and internal visions. What Dante sees comes to him as if in a gallery, and from Canto 8 on he observes and participates in the artistic ritual of the church, submitted to its range of didactic, emblematic, and allegorical offering as the means to this central stage of his reformation. The terraces of Purgatory are a divinely created visible rhetoric, in Dante's phrase "*visible par-lare*," designed to persuade the ambitious but still im-perfect and half-ignorant Christian soul to develop and change. Both the recording poet and the viewing pilgrim are confronted by sights and concepts increasingly dif-ficult to comprehend, and the human faculties must be strained and concentrated. Where the truth of nature begins to shade over into spiritual truth, the unaided human intellect falls short, but the mental processes involved in receiving and sorting out these truths once they have been set before the mind are similar to those required to grasp the world of created nature.[16] As we notice the reactions of Dante as spectator and pilgrim, we will see that his senses, emotions, and imagination are just as much in play as always, but with the difference that there is a greater frequency and intensity of specifically imaginative activity.

Bundy has argued that Dante is enough of a Platonist to embrace a dualism, indeed an antagonism, of matter and spirit alien to Scholastic thought and requiring two modes of imagination, one "a power giving shape to the presentations of the sense or of the memory" (*imaginativa*); the other "the power of imagination to aid intellect by constructing pictures for the guidance of more abstract processes of thought" (*fantasia*).[17] One power is located in the sensitive soul and records and reproduces material images from surrounding nature; the other is a rational faculty and fashions icons whose only status is to represent the immaterial that the human mind cannot grasp in its essence. Such a theory has some precedent in medieval thought,[18] but Dante's use of the two terms does not permit us this easy distinction. In the *Commedia* he does not begin to use *fantasia* until *Purgatorio* 17, but it is precisely in that Canto that both terms appear. In lines 13 and 21, *imaginativa* refers to the faculty, and in line 25 *fantasia* designates the content. But then so does *imagine* in line 31 and *imaginar* in line 43, and in *Vita Nuova* 39, Dante mentions *una forte imaginazione* in the same sense, not as in "I have a strong power of imagination," but "I experienced a powerful vision." Moreover, "imagination" and "fantasy" are both used in *Vita Nuova* 23 to indicate the false dream with which that canto and its lyric are concerned. Finally, in *Convivio* II, iv, *fantasia* refers to the faculty, not to what that faculty envisions; but when it appears in *Paradiso* 33. 142, the reference once again is to content. The differences Dante emphasizes are not in the human faculty of inner sight, which is protean rather than divided into two powers located separately in the soul, but in the nature of what the imagination sees and in the source. Examples of the kind of imagining that deals primarily with material surroundings occur in *Inferno* 23, where Dante and Virgil suppose that they are being pursued by the Malebranche (which shortly turns out to be the case) or in *Inferno* 31, where Dante thinks he can discern a city, a false conclusion he reaches from observing vague shapes half visible beyond the dimness. The immediate causes of such relatively simple visions are material and actual, just as the sight of Beatrice in *Vita Nuova*, Chapter 2, is the immediate source of her appearance to his imagination dressed in a red garment and carried in the arms of the god of love.

Dreams, daydreams, visions, and imaginings of a different origin occur in *Purgatorio*, and in Canto 17 Dante insists that these, like the carved images, are divinely inspired:

> Recall, reader, if ever in the mountains a mist has caught you, through which you could not see, except as moles do through the skin, how, when the moist dense vapors begin to dissipate, the sphere of the sun enters through them, and your fancy [*la tua imagine*] will quickly come to see how, at first, I saw the sun again, which was not at its setting. So, matching mine to the trusty steps of my master, I came forth from such a fog to the rays which were already dead on the low shores.
>
> O imagination, that do sometimes so snatch us from outward things that we give no heed, though a thousand trumpets sound around us, who moves you if the sense affords you naught? A light moves you which takes form in heaven, of itself, or by a will that downward guides it.

Of her impious deed who changed her form into the bird
that most delights to sing, the impress appeared in my
imagination, and at this my mind was so restrained within
itself, that from outside came naught that was then received
by it. Then rained down within the high fantasy [*Poi piovve
dentro a l'alta fantasia*] one crucified, scornful and fierce in his
mien, and so was he dying. (11. 1—27)[19]

This occurs in the circle where anger is purged. Dante's
rapt phantasy takes in three scenes, the two above concerning Procne and Haman and a third involving Amata
in the *Aeneid*. Embodying types of destructive hatred,
these scenes also testify to the pilgrim's capacity to
receive morally instructive pictures in a state of mind in
which the imagination is powerful and totally concentrated on a single image.

Dante is here once again the spectator (not the creating poet), seeking to involve the reader as urgently as he
can by asking him to imagine what imagination is like in
these circumstances. Is the reader's "fancy" (as Singleton translates) in line 7 meant to contrast utterly with the
imagination and "high fantasy" of lines 21 and 25? The
first is certainly concerned with a more or less commonplace experience, and the other two refer to visions
supplied through divine grace. Yet the contrast is not all
that absolute. Dante invites the reader to participate
"imaginatively" on the basis of his own possible experience and follows this by an account of something more
inward, concentrated, and exclusive, and yet, he hints,
the mental experiences are similar: obscurity giving way
to blazing, intense clarity. The Italian *imagine* is Dante's
word for the reader's faculty and for his own; *imaginativa*
refers to the faculty in general; *fantasia* translates the
particular vision Dante as pilgrim has undergone.

Canto 10, where the terrace of pride begins is the first section of *Purgatorio* openly to employ artistic didacticism and illustrates the connections Dante seeks to establish between art and the spectator's reactions. The canto begins by calling attention to the "gate which the souls' wrong love disuses, making the crooked way seem straight." The entrance to the road to salvation is little used because so many fix their affections on something other than God. By obeying the warder's command not to look back once he has passed through, Dante has begun to turn his eyes and his mind to divine things, and he and Virgil thread their way up the narrow ascent—"that needle's eye—until they wearily arrive at "a level place more solitary than roads through deserts." But almost at once Dante notices "that the encircling bank . . . was of pure white marble, and was adorned with such carvings that not only Polycletus but Nature herself would there be put to shame" (11. 1–33).

The carvings are drastically mimetic and so vivid that they seem to speak. Sculpture becomes, in the imagination of the spectator, literature, or better yet, drama. The Annunciation scene strikes Dante as "not a silent image" (1. 39). "One would have sworn that he [Gabriel] was saying, '*Ave*,' for there she was imaged who turned the key to open the supreme love, and these words were imprinted in her attitude: '*Ecce ancilla Dei*,' as expressly as a figure is stamped on wax" (11. 40–45). At the bidding of Virgil Dante looks beyond to the right and sees "another story set in the rock" ("un'altra storie ne la rocca imposta"), that of David dancing before the Ark. *Storie* is the correct word, for what Dante here describes are indeed "speaking pictures," capsule narratives, illustrative of humility and so intensely immediate to his senses that momentarily he is confused: "In front appeared people, and all the company, divided into seven choirs, made two of my senses say, the one 'No,' and the other, 'Yes, they are singing.' In like manner, by the smoke of the incense that was imaged there my eyes and my nose were made discordant with *yes* and *no*" (11. 58—63).

It is important that in each case the eyes are the organs of affirmation, and though their literal affirmation is quite wrong, we should not suppose that Dante is merely paying tribute to the powerfully illusionary excellence of divine mimesis. The act of viewing, which marks Dante's behavior all through the *Commedia*, is here insisted on rather pointedly: in the psychology of the poem the eyes are the most important avenue to understanding, and the imagination is primarily a faculty of internal or mental vision. Dante imagines the actuality of the scenes before him because the art he confronts is so superbly accomplished, and that accomplishment, beyond the capacity of human artist or of nature, helps to guarantee a proper response. The lesson in humility is almost self-evident: Dante notes that David appeared "both more and less than king," simultaneously falling beneath and exceeding in his self-abasement the worldly dignity of royalty.

The third carving, depicting an anecdote from the life of the emperor Trajan, provokes an even more detailed reaction.

I moved my feet from where I was to examine close at hand another story which I saw gleaming white beyond Michal. There storied was the high glory of the Roman prince whose worth moved Gregory to his great victory: I

mean the Emperor Trajan. And a poor widow was at his
bridle in an attitude of weeping and of grief. Round about
him appeared a trampling and throng of horsemen, and
above them the eagles in gold moved visibly in the wind.
Among all these the poor woman seemed to say, "My lord,
do me vengeance for my son who is slain, wherefore my
heart is pierced." And he seemed to answer her, "Wait now
till I return." And she, "My lord," like one whose grief is
urgent, "and if you do not return?" And he, "He who shall
be in my place will do it for you." And she, "What shall
another's well doing avail you, if you forget your own?" He
then, "Now take comfort, for I must discharge my duty
before I go: justice requires it, and pity bids me stay."

He who never beheld any new thing wrought this visible
speech, new to us because here it is not found. (11. 70—96)

It is Dante the spectator, as well as Dante the poet,
who supplies the dialogue, who turns the stone figures
into dramatic interlude. His reaction is not alone a
matter of reasoning. He imagines not the carvings,
which are perceived visibly and accessible to the external
senses, but the language that gives greater intellectual
clarity to the scene. Dante's response encompasses
several faculties and powers; the whole intellect seems
to be in play. But rational delight and moral comprehension seem to translate the quality of affect: "I was taking
delight in gazing on the images of humilities so great"
(11. 97—98).[20]

So far in this canto there is a fairly clear connection
between perfected mimetic art, the viewer's properly
functioning mind and feelings, and a concept of moral
virtue that is directly applicable to the condition of the
viewer's soul and consequent behavior. Dante reports
that these scenes in marble are executed with divine
skill, but they concern human attitudes and acts. We

might even suppose him to be positing a relationship between mimetic art and positive moral virtue, did he not establish just the same kind of link between the figured floor and examples of hatred in Canto 12. In any case, at the end of Canto 10 another connection between genre and subject matter does occur. Dante's delight in contemplating images of humility quite suddenly gives place to sympathetic anguish as he comes upon souls being punished for pride, and the transition to the direct opposite of delight is so absolute that he warns the reader, "Heed not the form of the pain: think what follows" (11. 109–110). But Dante the pilgrim does heed the form of the pain and describes it in some detail:

> As for corbel to support a ceiling or a roof, sometimes a figure is seen to join the knees to the breast—which, unreal, begets real distress in one who sees it—so fashioned did I see these when I gave good heed. They were truly more or less contracted according as they had more or less upon their backs; and he who showed the most suffering in his looks, seemed to say, weeping, "I can no more." (11. 130–139)

These are souls in the attitude of grotesques—distorted, grimacing figures of a type still visible on medieval buildings. The style of the grotesque is an exaggeration of the natural to convey a strong emotional impression—"la qual fa del non ver vera rancura nascere 'n chi la vede." Once again Dante supplies imagined speech. The figures here are not carvings, only reminiscent of carvings, reminding us that deliberately unrealistic art may be designed to procure an appropriate, a "true" response in the spectator.[21]

The kind and sequence of images in Canto 10 is important psychologically. The carved figures, in a style we might today call magic realism, are essentially literary, presenting archetypical events with immediacy and prompting a delight in the transcendent skill of their execution as well as an imaginative response that accompanies a proper interpretation of their meaning. The "real" figures, on the other hand, are reminiscent of art, and through that resemblance suggest a different level of response: sympathetic feeling. Art, as it were, prepares our sensibility by directing and schooling the affections, and this is accomplished in part through diminishing the distance between art and life from both directions.

Dante's reactions to what he has seen in Canto 10 are not limited to delight or pity. Canto 11 opens with the Lord's Prayer, uttered by the same bent and distorted souls of the proud, and his response persists and moves to a different level:

> Thus, praying good speed for them and for us, these shades were going under the burden, like that of which one sometimes dreams, unequally anguished all of them, wearily making their rounds on the first terrace, purging away the mists of the world. If there they always ask good for us, what for them can here be said or done, by those who have their will rooted in good? Truly we ought to help them wash away the stains they have borne hence, so that pure and light they may go forth into the starry wheels. (11. 25–36)

This is clearly the author's aside to his readers, but it can also be understood as part of the fiction in that it translates what ought to be the effect of perceived artistic representation on the will of the viewer, prompting him to an act of Christian love towards the suffering penitents. It is not enough to recognize humility and pride and to perceive feelingly the consequences of each: one must extend understanding beyond oneself to attitudes and acts of charity.

As if to reinforce Dante's concept of the affective and moral function of art, the great illuminator Oderisi comments on the fragility of earthly reputation:

"Cimabue thought to hold the field in painting, and now Giotto has the cry, so that the other's fame is dim; so has the one Guido taken from the other the glory of our tongue—and he perchance is born that shall chase the one and the other from the nest." (11. 94–99)

This scene is part of Dante's effort to establish for art, and perhaps for his own art, its proper value: considered as the organ of the artist's self-aggrandizement and renown, it is fragile and transient ("Earthly fame is naught but a breadth of wind," 1. 100); what is of continuing worth is the influence of the work on the audience seeking salvation. Properly conceived and properly viewed, art incarnates the virtues to be acquired and the vices to be purged.

Canto 12 demonstrates this concept in a sustained and deliberately formal manner, but what is prominent is not so much the meaning of the images as the pilgrim's response to them:

As, in order that there be memory of them, the stones in the church floor over the buried dead bear figured what they were before; wherefore many a time men weep for them there, at the prick of memory that spurs only the faithful: so I saw sculptured there, but of a better semblance in respect of skill, all that for pathway juts out from the mountain. (11. 16–24)

Such gravestones still crowd the floors of medieval and
Renaissance churches, and their purpose was indeed to
refresh the memory and kindle the emotions of the
living faithful. What such a reaction might be emerges
from the rhetoric of the pilgrim as he lists the archetypes
of fallen pride, beginning with Lucifer—"I saw, on the
one side, him who was created nobler than any other
creature" (11. 25–26)—and ending with Troy:

> I saw Troy in ashes and in caverns: O Ilion, how cast
> down and vile it showed you—the sculpture that is there
> discerned. (11.61–63)

Once again Dante pays tribute to the surpassing skill
and lifelike power of divine art and concludes with a bit
of ironic moralizing:

> What master was he of brush or of pencil who drew the
> forms and lineaments which there would make every subtle
> genius wonder? Dead the dead, and the living seemed alive.
> He who saw the reality of all I trod upon, while I bent down,
> saw not better than I!
> Now wax proud, and on with haughty visage, you chil-
> dren of Eve, and bend not down your face to see your evil
> path! (11. 64–69)

All the several strands of Dante's demonstration of the
affective uses of art gathered into this scene from Canto
12: once again we are reminded of the churchly presence
and of the conditions of faith and cleared memory
necessary to read the graven lesson. The intensity of the
poetic voice and the charged formality of the language
betray the pilgrim's complete absorption and intensely
directed emotion—directed at one's own pride as well as

at the scenes of humiliated greatness. His mind, Dante says, is captive: "l'animo non sciolto" (1. 75); its release, we are meant to understand, is in the moralizing outburst, which is not only aimed at us, but expresses what has happened in the will and intellect of the pilgrim. Memory preserves the effigies of shattered pride; a superhuman invention brings the figures to the vividness of "reality"; and, properly disposed, the sensibility of the viewer, ranging from perception through imagination to intelligence and will, is utterly bound up in the study of the work of art. Something of the obsessive hunger of the lover in the *Vita Nuova* survives in Dante's role as spectator here. The act of gazing, externally and internally, is concentrated and exclusive. Things outside momentarily fade from consciousness and within the mind a broader world, full of holy and dreadful significance, comes alive. Something like this happens again in Canto 18 after Virgil's lecture on desire and free will. Dante's attention becomes abstracted, not once, but twice (11. 87, 139−145), and if we recall Virgil's point that attention amounts to desire, we will notice that the poem is acting out the play of imagination and appetite in Dante's dream of the siren in Canto 19.

The dream, the middle of three in *Purgatorio*, amounts to a fairly obvious lesson about the potential freedom of the imagination. The siren, at first "stammering, with eyes asquint and crooked on her feet, with maimed hands and sallow hue," is transformed from ugliness into an image of desirable beauty by the dreamer's gaze. We are meant, I think, to observe the power of imagination over will. Once the siren has sung and offered her delusive satisfactions, another lady, "holy and alert" appears and asks Virgil (who is present in the dream),

"Who is this?" Virgil unmasks the siren, and Dante is awakened by the stench that emerges from her belly. Later Virgil explains that the dream illustrates how man is freed from that "ancient witch," carnal love. The holy and alert lady may be read as the God-given power to distinguish good and evil, and Virgil, in the dream, functions as the "free" will that acts at the direction of enlightened moral discernment.[22] Here, as throughout the *Purgatorio*, the pilgrim is exhibited in a state of joint dependence on his own mental powers and divine grace. The occasion is one that shows up the false enchantments of the flesh, but its less obvious and perhaps more important point is to convey something about the natural or spontaneous power of the imagination. Left to itself imagination can transform moral ugliness into something delusive and compelling. Indirectly, then, Dante's requirement of the imagery of divine and churchly art, which offers things as they really are, is nicely underlined.

Severe limitations are thus imposed on the imagination, and indeed on the natural reason. Dante has earlier been quite capable of managing the clear example of humility, pride, and envy, at least to the extent of understanding them for what they are: the images on the figured terrace are, for example, unequivocal. But the dreams and much of the pageantry of *Purgatorio* require clarification either from Virgil or Beatrice or one of the other figures, and once Virgil abandons Dante in Canto 30, the poem has entered almost wholly into the realm of divine mystery, where images no longer declare their meanings by their appearance. Like the later critics to be examined in succeeding chapters, Dante is partisan to the doctrine of vividness in the affective function of art, but he is committed to a greater intricacy and difficulty in doctrine, with the result that the knowledge to be gained from the presentations of art becomes increasingly complicated.

The evident differences between the kinds of knowledge available in *Inferno*, *Pugatorio*, and *Paradiso*, as well as the distinctions apparent within the *Purgatorio*, appear to derive from a concept of the varying nature of substances combined with a theory of varying modes of cognition. Francis X. Newman has argued that Dante is following Augustine's *De Genesi ad Litteram*, Book XII, which distinguishes three modes of knowing, by means of the eye (which discerns objects of material substance); the imagination (which sees things with material shape but not material substance); and the intellect (which knows directly such immaterial realities as God, the angels, and love):

Whatever man knows he knows in one of these three ways, but Augustine is particularly interested in how we know God. In this regard he asserts that man can know God by means of any of the three visions: Moses gazing on the burning bush "saw" God with corporeal sight; John in the Apocalyptic vision saw Him by means of the figures and images of the *visio spiritualis*; and St. Paul's *raptus* [2 Corinthians, 12:2—4] is the great exemplar of the *visio intellectualis*. Only the last, however, is a direct intuition of God Himself; the others are indirect visions by means of bodies or images. While he speaks of three different visions, moreover, Augustine is also at pains to emphasize that vision is essentially a continuum, in which corporeal, spiritual, and intellectual vision are related in a hierarchical system. In normal human experience, that is to say, sensation is primary, but its data are transformed into and stored as the phantasms of imagination, and these in turn are the material form from which are drawn the imageless ideas of intellectual vision.[23]

Newman applies the Augustinian system primarily to the culminating visions of each *cantico*: at the bottom of Hell is the weighty figure of Satan in ironic reverse imitation of God; the apocalyptic pageant in Eden represents God incarnate; only at the end of *Paradiso* in the Empyrean is God confronted in His essence.

This reading is persuasive as a way of categorizing these three moments in the *Commedia*; it is perhaps somewhat less exact in discriminating among different modes of mental experience within each *cantico*, in part because differences in kinds of image, as well as in modes of seeing, are at issue. "The inhabitants of Purgatory," Newman continues, "are taught the nature of their sins by contemplating historical instances of the vice itself and its opposing virtue. Though drawn from Biblical and secular history, there is no sense in which these events are witnessed by the pilgrims as actual occurrences. They are *exempla*, the visual or auditory representation of events for didactic purposes."[24] Yet, as we have seen, Dante has made some effort to insist on their "actuality" in terms of the quality of affect they elicit from the spectator, and the sequence of Canto 10, in which what is seen moves from the carvings to the bent and distorted penitents and elicits a movement from one level of emotion to another, implies a rather more subtle interplay between bodily and imaginative sight than simple didacticism would encompass.

There are further distinctions. For example, the images of humility depict that virtue in action, in human terms, but they do not in themselves, in their pictorial or

sensory character, pretend to analyze the "causes" by
which it is justified or established as part of a larger
moral system. Similarly, the appearance of the penitents
on the terrace of pride or the envious with their eyelids
wired shut does not inform us of the reasons why pride
and envy occur. Such matters are left to direct discourse.[25] The allegorical pageants, as well as the three
prophetic dreams, are yet another issue, for they collect
into their imagery an intellectual context of broader
scope. Thus Dante's dream of Leah and Rachel is an
emblem of the nature of the active and contemplative
lives and a foretaste of the state of the ordered soul
which is to be more completely represented in Eden.[26]
And the sustained pageant of the Apocalypse which
occupies the final cantos of *Purgatorio* involves Dante
and the reader in still more complex and far-reaching
doctrine, though little verbal rationalization of the sym-
bols is offered.[27] At the same time, we have not moved
beyond the visual, consciously artistic vision. Dante
describes its beginnings as a canvas:

> When I was at a point on my bank where only the stream
> Lethe separated me, I held my steps in order to see better,
> and I saw the flames advance, leaving the air behind them
> painted, and they looked like moving paint brushes, so that
> overhead it remained streaked with seven bands in all those
> colors whereof the sun makes his bow, and Delia her girdle.
> (Canto 29, 11. 70–78)

It is not my purpose here to discuss interpretations of
the symbolism of Eden. It is often assumed that medieval readers would be more readily familiar than we are
with the symbolic meanings attached to the Griffon, the

chariot, the dancing ladies, the candlesticks, and so on; no doubt this is so. In the context of this book it is important to note that the pageant is more than a spectacle Dante views and interprets, for it surrounds Beatrice's stern accusations about the errors of his former life (Canto 30, 11. 58–145), his confession (Canto 31, 11. 31–46), and his subsequent witness to the prophetic recapitulation of the history and meaning of man's fall and redemption (Cantos 31–33) which concludes *Purgatorio*. The pilgrim, and by extension the reader he brings with him, cannot rightly view the pageant unless it is involved in the correction of his own will, and even then understanding is difficult. In a pointed reference to the *Vita Nuova*, Beatrice underlines the failure of Dante's power of vision and the misdirection of his love after her death:

"Not only through the working of the great wheels, which direct every seed to some end according as the stars are its companions, but through largess of divine graces, which have for their rain vapors so lofty that our sight goes not near thereto, this man was such in his new life, virtually, that every right disposition would have made marvelous proof in him. But so much more rank and wild becomes the land, ill-sown and untilled, as it has more of good strength of soil. For a time I sustained him with my countenance: showing him my youthful eyes I led him with me turned toward the right goal. So soon as I was on the threshold of my second age and had changed life, this one took himself from me and gave himself to others. When from flesh to spirit I had ascended, and beauty and virtue were increased in me, I was less dear and less pleasing to him and he turned his steps along a way not true, following false images of good, which pay no promise in full. Nor did it avail me to

> obtain inspirations with which, both in dream and other-
> wise I called him back, so little did he heed them. He fell
> so low that all the means for his salvation were now short,
> save to show him the lost people." (Canto 30, 11. 109–138)

In reviewing Dante's life before *Purgatorio*, this passage
expresses the central dramatic motive of the *Commedia*
and links it by reference to false images of good to the essays on desire in *Purgatorio* 16–18. Hell has exhibited the
fatal results of misdirected desire, and against this Beatrice's eyes become both a collective image of beauty to be
desired and the medium for true understanding. In
Canto 31, having confessed and been carried by Matelda
across Lethe, Dante is brought before the Griffon where
Beatrice attends him, and he reports:

> A thousand desires hotter than flame held my eyes on the
> shining eyes that remained ever fixed on the Griffon. As the
> sun in a mirror, so was the twofold animal gleaming there-
> within, now with the one, now with the other bearing.
> Think, reader, if I marveled when I saw the thing stand still
> in itself, and in its image changing. (11. 118–126)

The Griffon represents the mystery of the divine and
human aspects of Christ, and Beatrice (whose symbolic
import is multiple in the poem) has referred to the
human and spiritual in herself. We are presented here
with icons of the quality of knowledge or illumination
which man should desire and seek, and with a further
suggestion of the difficulties in "seeing" correctly. Sin-
fulness may prevent man from fixing his eyes and his
affections on the appropriate images, but even when his
error has been purged and his will made free, the natural
limitations of the human mind still obtain and the

mediation of Beatrice, of grace to assist contemplation, is still necessary to the viewing of divine mystery.

Dante's concept of the usefulness of art is thus something more than a simple Horatian doctrine of profitability. It involves first of all the proposition that knowledge is required for salvation; second, the further proposition that the development of the power to see correctly must be gradual and progressive (with the corollary that this development can be frustrated by misdirected affections); and third, a sense that knowledge is hierarchical. Broadly speaking that hierarchy extends from the natural world and the conditions of man's ethical existence to the mysteries of divine intervention and purpose in the world, and beyond these to questions of the essence of the divine. Both the material and spiritual are accessible to the mind, the material more easily of course and the spiritual through the gift of grace. Grace is necessary in part because, as Dante has told us, man's imagination does not match his power of speech and his power of speech is inferior to his intellectual grasp. Nevertheless, without the imagination nothing at all would be intelligible and the human will would lack objects of desire. The imagination has the special capacity to embody the spiritual or intelligible in material form and, as a bridge between the senses and the intellect, it permits us to join emotion to understanding. In the phrase, "a thousand desires hotter than flame held my eyes on the shining eyes," there is a clue to the persistent materiality of the *Commedia*. For Dante knowledge is not a dispassionate intellectual grasp of propositions, because what is worth knowing (and only knowledge pertinent to salvation is worth knowing, even though that encompasses a great deal) must be entertained by the whole sensibility. The urge to dispel ignorance is therefore much more than simple inquisitiveness; it is a passionate craving about things of consequence to one's own destiny. And the satisfaction of this desire is like the basest sensory pleasure: ". . . my soul, full of amazement and gladness, was tasting of that food which, sating of itself, causes hunger for itself," Dante says as he describes his concentration upon the changing image of the Griffon (Canto 30, 11. 127–129).

Dante's insistence on seeing, on imagining, on the affective signs of bodily sensation is of course rhetorical. His aim as poet is to make the experience of his vision as sharply immediate, as vivid in the literal sense of the term, as he can. His readers must imagine that they are there with him. But the pilgrim's desire for knowledge and the manner in which he acquires it are also aspects of the soul's longing for God, so that the employment of the imagery of sensation in the *Commedia* has a double purpose, to recapitulate literal physical experiences with which we are all familiar as a way to make the fictional experience humanly believable and to translate what it is like to reach for and enjoy spiritual knowledge.

The use of imagery to convey the experience of divine truth becomes, as many students of Dante have testified, more problematic in the *Paradiso*. Here the relationship between the image and what it translates becomes wholly that which Dante had begun to develop in the later cantos of the *Purgatorio*: truth is only imperfectly recovered because the human mind cannot readily formulate what it has experienced in the realms of heaven. In Canto 1 of the *Paradiso* Dante asks for divine assistance to "show forth the *image* of the blessed realm which is imprinted in my mind" (lines 24–25).[28] The

vision he reports is miraculous and beyond ordinary
human expression, and as pilgrim he can only experience heavenly realities vicariously through the medium
of the gaze of Beatrice fastened directly on the sun.
Indeed he tells us that the quality of what he saw even at
second hand is so far beyond his power of direct communication that he must resort to homely and familiar
sensations:

> I did not endure it long, nor so little that I did not see it
> sparkle round about, like iron that comes molten from the
> fire. And suddenly day seemed added to day, as if He who
> has the power had adorned heaven with another sun.
> Gazing upon her I became within me such as Glaucus
> became on tasting of the grass that made him sea-fellow of
> the other gods. The passing beyond humanity may not be
> set forth in words: therefore let the example suffice any for
> whom grace reserves that experience. (Canto 1, 11. 58–72)

There is some exaggeration here, since Dante does
make the effort to set forth the experience in words, but
the words are "images" or shadows of the reality they
attempt to render in a way that perhaps they have not
been before. In the *Inferno* and *Purgatorio* what the
pilgrim sees is what is there, so reality, vision, and
language are understood to be coordinate. In the *Paradiso*
until the very end vision is proximate to reality, but not
identical with it. Dante's apology suggests not only a
greater distance between language and reality but between language and the pilgrim's vision, so that the
experience of the unearthly can only be suggested by
insisting upon the impossibility of suggesting it truly.
For one critic, Marguerite Chiarenza, Dante's effort is to

convey through imagery an "imageless vision."[29] According to this formulation, however difficult the various experiences in the *Purgatorio*, they were composed of palpable sights, visible images designed by God to instruct the soul in the process of redemption. Art, we might say, constitutes the sensible reality of the *Purgatorio*. But in the *Paradiso*, beyond the earth (for Eden after all is a *place* on earth), there is little sensible reality except the planetary spheres. It is not so much a place as a state of being, and there images are only present as an illusion or shadow of its reality because they are the only terms in which man can even approximate an understanding.[30] Professor Chiarenza argues that "the basic position of the poet in the *Paradiso* is revealed by his struggle to express a vision which was imageless from the start," and insists that "we must stress the declared superhuman quality of vision in these cantos and do away with definitions, such as *per speculum* or *in aenigmate*, which make of it nothing more than a rarefied version of human experience."[31]

At this point it is well to return to what we have already seen of Dante's views of the human capacity for vision. On the one hand he has said that the intellect, once it is freed from the material, can receive the "divine light," and on the other he has testified to the limits of human imagination in our effort to apprehend "perfectly" and communicate knowledge of "substances separate from matter." Imagination supplies "the language of signs," but its weakness it not simply that it is incapable of some rendering of what is beyond mortal experience but that it prevents perfect and complete apprehension. Dante's effort, throughout the *Commedia*, has been to lead the reader to imagine what the afterlife is like, but this is not a single, knowable experience. It is instead a set of connected and ordered experiences involving different and progressively more difficult and universalized perspectives. We must imagine what "substances separate from matter" are like, or what it is like to be among them and know them, and at the same time suppose that because we are limited to imagining, rather than direct knowing, the terms in which the "ineffable" is communicated to us have no real or "mimetic" relationship to it. Everything expressed in the *Paradiso* is metaphor, even the literal level of the poem, and it is a metaphor somewhat different in kind from the metaphor of the journey through *Inferno* and *Purgatorio*, for there is the suggestion through much of these that their "essence" can be apprehended more accurately. It is not until the *Paradiso* that Dante openly confesses that what he is presenting to the reader must necessarily fall far short of what was actually there.

An essential aspect of my thesis has been the close identity between Dante as pilgrim and spectator and the reader. Professor Chiarenza, in order to support her argument for the "imageless vision" suggests the disappearance of the dimension of time in the *Paradiso*, and a consequently different relationship between poet and pilgrim. "In fact, while the pilgrim is speeding through the heavens at a velocity inconceivable to the human mind, time for the poet, the length of the third *cantica*, is the same as it was in the other two. This consideration leads us to confront the new relationship between the pilgrim and the poet. . . . In the *Paradiso* it is the poet who struggles while the pilgrim is safe. . . . Human categories of perception were left behind with Purga-

tory."[32] She adds in a note that "the poetics of the
Paradiso become much clearer if we remove the presence
of images from the pilgrim's vision and consider them to
exist only in the poet's."[33] But this is a mistake in part:
true enough the fiction of Paradise, the supposition that
a mortal could, even if momentarily, taste beatitude,
requires that we suppose the pilgrim to have had an
"imageless vision," but the text does not support the
contention that this obtains through the whole of the
Paradiso. There is ample indication that this is what the
pilgrim moves towards and that hence the process of his
seeing is one of gradual emancipation from the need to
imagine, as well as to express, everything in images that
are less than accurate reflections of the reality behind
them. For one thing, at the beginning of each successive
stage of "seeing" Dante must focus his vision through
the eyes of Beatrice until at length she leaves him in
Canto 31.[34] More pointed perhaps is the explanation in
Canto 4 which she offers of the apparent presence of
redeemed souls, prophets, angels, and the Virgin Mary
in the realms of the various planets below the Empyrean.
They

> "have not their seats in any other heaven than these spirits
> which have now appeared to you, nor have they more or
> fewer years for their existence; but all make the first circle
> beautiful, and have sweet life in different measure, by feel-
> ing more and less the eternal breath. These showed them-
> selves here, not because this sphere is allotted to them, but
> to afford sign of the celestial grade that is least exalted. It is
> needful to speak thus to your faculty, since only through
> sense perception does it apprehend that which it afterwards
> makes fit for the intellect. For this reason Scripture con-
> descends to your capacity, and attributes hands and feet to

God, having other meaning; and Holy Church represents
to you with human aspect Gabriel and Michael and the
other who made Tobit whole again." (11. 30—48)[35]

It is important that in line 40 Beatrice says "your faculty"
(*vostra ingegno*," which might better be translated "your
wit"), and again in line 44 she refers to "*vostra facultate*,"
thus reminding Dante that he is still a mortal and
preserving the link between the imagination of the
pilgrim and that of the reader. Though the conclusion of
the *Commedia* is susceptible to various interpretations,
the way in which the vision of the Trinity is phrased
suggests that only for a moment, which Dante does not
even attempt to describe, was his vision lifted beyond its
habit of seeing in images.

> That circling which, thus begotten, appeared in Thee as
> reflected light, when my eyes dwelt on it for a time, seemed
> to me depicted with our image within itself and in its own
> color, wherefore my sight was entirely set upon it.
>   As is the geometer who wholly applies himself to measure
> the circle, and finds not, in pondering, the principle of
> which he is in need, such was I at that new sight. I wished
> to see how the image conformed to the circle and how it has
> its place therein; but my own wings were not sufficient for
> that, save that my mind was smitten by a flash wherein its
> wish came to it. Here power failed the lofty phantasy; but
> already my desire and my will were revolved, like a wheel
> that is evenly moved, by the Love which moves the sun and
> the other stars. (Canto 33, 11. 127—145)

The flash, the brief gift of insight, does not last. What
Dante saw as a result of the flash, he does not really
attempt to recapture. Prior to that moment he saw

images, and the poet, in attempting to recreate even these, suffers from inadequate memory (Canto 1) and speech "feeble to [his] conception" (Canto 33).[36]

What Dante does convey is the sense in which Paradise, the heavens, the Empyrean, and the final vision of the Trinity are to be understood as images of art, so that however difficult it is for the human imagination and intellect to conceive them and however much they surpass these sights available in Purgatory and Eden, they must nevertheless be thought of as if they were made by the supreme artist. So Canto 10, which concerns the sphere of the sun, begins:

> Looking up on His Son with the Love which the One and the Other eternally breathe forth, the primal and ineffable Power made everything that revolves through the mind or through space with such order that he who contemplates it cannot but taste of Him. Lift then your sight with me, reader, to the lofty wheels, straight to that part where the one motion strikes the other; and amorously there begin to gaze upon that Master's art who within Himself so loves it that His eye never turns from it. (11. 1–12)

This is a noble and heartening view of the system of things, a tribute to divine artistry and by inference a tribute to the human art that attempts to encourage man to see in this fashion. Yet it would be mistaken not to understand the degree to which Dante's union of imaginative vision and the possibility of redemption requires the intervention of God. The imagination of the artist, even in the early stages of Purgatory where the work of art becomes a noticeable and even formidable part of the viewer's environment, needs the supplement of grace.

There is more than a casual implication that the mind of
the spectator and reader must also be initially disposed
towards salvation. Given these not inconsiderable conditions, then art can penetrate the imagination and by
stages draw the will, the capacity to gaze amorously on
good things, to objects we ought to deplore, pity,
admire, or covet. By thus engaging the emotions and the
mind this divine art teaches us what they are and where
they may lead us. The *Purgatorio* is an intermediate stage
in the education of the soul, but it is a most important
stage. It takes in the transition from the sights and
sounds of material nature, the sweet light Dante immediately notices on emerging from Hell, to the more
ordered and crafted level of art, that aspect of divinity
available to the aspiring soul in this life which disciplines
our feelings and understanding in preparation for mysteries only accessible to faith. From one point of view the
Purgatorio is the journey of the mind to the outer edges
of reason, but at the same time it narrates what the
proper direction of the mind should be: toward the habit
of proper appetite. It is here that Dante prepares us for
the didactic theory of the Renaissance.

III

Universals and Particulars: Fracastoro and Barbaro

When Girolamo Fracastoro and Daniele Barbaro were writing towards the middle of the sixteenth century, the intellectual climate for critics had altered. The complex and dominant theological system that circumscribed and included Dante's account of the influence of art upon the well-disposed will no longer dictated the declared purposes of fictional discourse: two centuries of the efforts of Humanist apology for literature—one thinks especially of Petrarch, Boccaccio, and Salutati—had urged that poetry, even and especially pagan poetry, was supreme among the arts of language. Rather than present the fictional image as an aid to salvation, Fracastoro and Barbaro make their arguments in an intellectual world in which it could be seen in competition with philosophy and history and in which its use could be measured either in terms of knowledge more perfectly displayed or of moral instruction aimed at behavior.

The two critics complement each other. Both are influenced by Neoplatonic thought in understanding the artistic image as embodying ideal or universal forms; both subscribe to a psychology derived from Aristotle. Where they differ is in emphasis: Fracastoro is primarily interested in how the mind proceeds from sensory experience to intellectual understanding; Barbaro echoes this interest but focuses more consistently on the affective properties of language. Together they exemplify a stage in Italian sixteenth-century theory prior to that which saw close examination of questions of genre or of what constitutes a "true" poem. Their overriding purpose is to examine poetry and language at large.

FRACASTORO

Three of Fracastoro's works concern us, the dialogues *Naugerius, sive de Poetica; Turrius, sive de Intellectione;* and *Fracastorius, sive de Anima.*[1] Their subjects are poetry, thinking, and the nature of the soul. Internal references indicated that they were conceived as related and partially interdependent, and taken together they show a persistent concern with the ways in which the mind and its capacity to entertain images bring universal and particular together in morally intelligible expression. Fracastoro reveals an interest in Platonism, but his epistemology is, as Hathaway indicates, in substantial debt to Aristotle, especially in one of his major premises, that the particulars of sensory perception are the necessary counters of conceptual thinking: "Chiefly, Fracastoro, like Aristotle, developed a system of mind in which all forms of thought are developed immediately or mediately from sense impressions and in which there is no appreciable gulf between the sense shape of things and abstract ideas. Imagination, consequently, was an important part of mind."[2]

Fracastoro argues that thought is to be understood as the presence of the appearance or simulacra of things in the mind. The mind responds passively to matter, but actively construes form. Furthermore, everything the mind can understand can be represented by intelligible "appearances." These can occur within the mind and be retained. In other words, the mind may in some instances fashion images revealing essences or truths by virtually translating appearances, and this theory is important for the light it throws on the poet's capacity to invent.[3] However, the central issue is not the idea of a thing or object:

> But the principal problem remained—how does the mind move from sense images, organized or unorganized, into abstractions? . . . We have knowledge of some things that are not known in themselves but are apprehended through other "appearances." These, of course, are immaterial, and though they may be represented by images (or appearances) they do not actually have the properties of those images which serve to represent them. There may be a "similitude" between the image and the immateriality it represents, but whatever in the image approximates the material is not a necessary property of the immaterial thing. Images may be avenues to the knowledge of what they represent, but they are not part of it. The connection of similitude between image and essence is work of imagination.[4]

This analysis is of *Turrius*, the dialogue on thinking, and Hathaway looks to it for its application to the creative poetic process. There is also considerable relevance to the process of the reader's understanding. In *Turrius* Fracastoro does not face the artistic and affective issues directly, but *Naugerius*, his poetics, seeks to encompass the work of the poet, the nature of the poem, and the quality and purpose of the poem's impact on the reader. Arguments that were to surface in Sidney's emphatic plea for the supremacy of poetry as an instrument to persuade the soul are here offered in a form that makes Fracastoro's epistemology necessary to their validity.

Naugerius essentially answers objections that poetry, though pleasing, is a superficial divertissement. Those answers centrally involve the poet's ability to find and represent universality. "While others consider the particular, the poet considers the universal. So the others are like the painter who represents the features and other members of the body as they really are in the object; but the poet it like the painter who does not wish to represent this or that particular man as he is with many defects, but who, having contemplated the universal and supremely beautiful idea of his creator, makes things as they ought to be."[5] Particulars deviate from the pattern or model, and in this deviation lies their individuality. Thus it is the absence of the deviant individuality which the poet seeks to represent.

Furthermore, those things the poet imitates pertain, insofar as they are objects of contemplation, to the will, "since they can produce wisdom and other virtues. . . . Consequently, because the poet seeks the noblest and most beautiful elements in each subject, it follows that poetry will display more of those qualities which pertain to wisdom and the other virtues. For the same reason, if the poet imitates the things which belong to the intellect he will teach more because he omits no beauty which can be attributed to things. . . ."[6] This poetics of rationality does not yet reach far enough into the topic to explain precisely by what means the poet touches the will nor does it explain how the poet might differ from the philosopher.

"The things which belong to the intellect" are those that merit the attention of the mind and are accessible to it, and, as Fracastoro has mentioned earlier, "If the poet imitates nature as well as people, it will seem indeed that his whole purpose has been made complete, by producing practical knowledge through the imitation of people, and perceptive knowledge through the imitation of natural objects, in which he will imitate what is perfect and excellent in things."[7] Otherwise, he does not wish to limit the poet (or, for that matter, the orator or historian), for "Every subject is proper to the poet so long as he can adorn it."[8]

For Fracastoro, then, the crucial question is mode of treatment, or in the terms he uses, adornment. In discussing this aspect of poetry, he understands style in a broad sense to include what is fictive in a poem. Quoting a passage from the *Georgics* ("Or where some grove / Dark with thick oaks lies in sacred shadow" [III, ii, 333–334]), he says, "Observe with what beauties he paints the woods, adding 'lies,' and 'dark with thick oaks,' and 'in sacred shadow.' " This is speaking "simply and in accordance with the universal idea of eloquence," and except for the poet, "all others who strive for eloquence . . . imitate the particular, that is the object exactly as it is. The poet imitates not the particular but the simple idea clothed in its own beauties, which Aristotle calls the universal."[9] With a wave of the wand

Fracastoro turns Aristotle into something of a Platonist, but the interesting point is that ornament or descriptive imagery translates the universal. Furthermore, the same feature of poetic art is what impresses the reader and arouses his admiration, and in this justification of ornament there is a parallel to Fracastoro's views in *Turrius* and *De Anima* that images may be the means to knowledge of something to which they do not naturally belong.

The capacity of the poet or painter to embody universals that are better than observable particulars, to fashion patterns that things in the phenomenal world may point to but cannot precisely reach or resemble, must be matched by the reader's or spectator's ability to cross the same mental bridge between the particular and the universal, or to recognize that images express universals, rather than particulars. Like the poet, he too must be able to regard the poetic or painted image as a sign of the ideal. The quality of this mental capacity appears more specifically in Fracastoro's *De Anima*. He approaches the topic in the customary way by comparing the human to the angelic mind in terms of their relative abilities to know the universal or immaterial. By divine grace angels enjoy the supreme felicity of knowing God directly and immediately (and here we are in territory reminiscent of Aquinas and Dante), and in discussing the nature of the divine mind, he makes plain the difference between human and godly knowledge: "Christ surrendered to a most perfect knowing of himself, a knowledge, however, not so much through the species and simulacra of things, as other men know, but through the proper substance of God himself, in which knowledge beatitude consists."[10] Fracastoro does not really argue the issue of whether the immaterial is the universal idea to which all particulars belong and by which they have reference to each other or whether there is some more radical disjunction between the phenomenal and the noumenal. Rather he is interested in making plain his view that the only way the human mind can know the immaterial is by means of the material. Although man's intellect does not have a material form, it can think only through images derived from matter and expressed by the senses, "the species and simulacra of things."[11]

The relationship of the mind to these species is interesting. The soul or intellect is both active and passive. Where material objects are concerned it is passive, but where form is concerned the soul is active. It seeks out form, but does so only upon passively receiving the object into the mind through the senses. Once this has occurred, the mind can recast or recreate forms, a step beyond simply receiving impressions. Once impressions have entered the mind, the common sense relates them to appearances from other senses. Then what Fracastoro calls "subnotion" takes over.[12] He is working towards the proposition that human intellection is impossible without the presence of material images. Either the mind perceives material objects and receives their species or simulacra, or, in order to think clearly about abstractions or the immaterial, it uses simulacra to represent them.

The manner in which the mind moves from species or simulacra to those things that objectively lack them is twofold. First of all intensity and repetition are required. "Just as one more intense light results from two lights, so from two, three, or ten species a single, more intense one results: made more intense both by being spread

among many spirits and by being fixed more deeply."[13]
In the second place, Fracastoro considers how the mind
knows those things that lack species or material properties and how it invents or abstracts and separates those
things that are joined and joins those that are separate.
Those things that lack species are "known" through the
species of other things. In other words what we could
call the context of generality is imagined by postulating
similarity or difference. Thus an idea is formed by the
process of repetition and by an almost arbitrary act of
borrowing the attributes of a material thing to guess at
the nature of an immaterial thing.

> Therefore, those things which have no kind of species and
> are not joined to substances are all known by means of other
> species, and when we first conceive them they are imagined
> by similitude or dissimilitude to things or objects. Then,
> attributing to them certain similarities or dissimilarities
> found in other things, we form an idea of them. So we know
> God and other material things, and substance itself. Since
> indeed we know what first is, what a mover is, and what
> corporeal is, we say that God is the first cause and prime
> mover and incorporeal.[14]

For Fracastoro these movements of the mind from
material to immaterial things by means of "similitudes
and dissimilitudes" are the essential work of the imagination. A modern philosopher might argue that in the
statement just quoted Fracastoro is simply combining
words in an arbitrary manner and that the process of
comparison and contrast can only work between things
already known in some degree: one cannot by this
method proceed from the perceived to the impercepti-
ble, though one can certainly conceive an idea of the

immaterial and unknown. But Fracastoro does not ask
such questions. Perhaps assuming as most thinkers did
in the Renaissance a given relationship between nature
and God, he regards the method to be valid. In any case,
for him the imagination amounts to creating contexts,
groupings, and connections within the mind which are
not necessarily evident to the senses. "The soul," he
asserts, "is even able to admit separate things as joined
by their similitudes; first it sees them as joined and then
it separates them. Excited by a certain pleasure derived
from this similitude, it imagines those things which are
separate as joined, either by place, subject, or something
else. By this means it fashions for itself chimeras and
centaurs, and just so the poet makes gardens and
palaces."[15] Furthermore, in discussing abstractions that
may derive from divine or other sources, Fracastoro
insists that they will nevertheless present themselves to
the mind as phantasms sorted through the same mental
processes as the images of material things.

The crucial statement from *Naugerius* that the poet
"makes" for himself a simple, beautiful, universal idea
can now be understood more precisely: in *Turrius* abstraction is described as in part a denuding of the
particulars that cling to an object in order to get at an
essence; this essence is then represented in the mind by
phantasms. If one wishes to represent justice, one has
the two objects, a man and justice. In combining them so
that the first represents the second, one does not represent a particular man, warts and all. Rather one represents a man shorn of all particularities except those that
may refer to the idea of justice. The material images that
remain are sorted through the mind according to the
same sequence by which a sensible particular reaches

the level of rational contemplation.[16]

What this dependence upon images derived from material particulars seems to imply is that the mind does not start with a concept of the immaterial which has no imaginal content and then clothe it with images. Rather the immaterial universal is approached generally through particulars that at a certain stage of intellection are no longer contemplated for themselves but used to represent things they in themselves are not. This form of representation is what Fracastoro means by invention, and the paradigm of the theory is to be found in Cicero's *Orator* where he endeavors to illustrate the usefulness of the ideal:

> Consequently in delineating the perfect orator I shall be portraying such a one as perhaps has never existed. Indeed I am not inquiring who was the perfect orator, but what is that unsurpassable ideal which seldom if ever appears throughout a whole speech but does shine forth at some times and in some places, more frequently in some speakers, more rarely perhaps in others. But I am firmly of the opinion that nothing of any kind is so beautiful as not to be excelled in beauty by that of which it is a copy, as a mask is a copy of a face. This ideal cannot be perceived by the eye or ear, nor by any of the senses, but we can nevertheless grasp it by the mind and the imagination. For example, in the case of the statues of Phidias, the most perfect of their kind that we have ever seen, and in the case of the paintings I have mentioned, we can, in spite of their beauty, imagine something more beautiful. Surely that great sculptor, while making the image of Jupiter or Minerva, did not look at any person whom he was using as a model, but in his own mind there dwelt a surpassing vision of beauty; at this he gazed and all intent on this he guided his artist's hand to

produce the likeness of god. Accordingly, as there is something perfect and surpassing in the case of sculpture and
painting—an intellectual ideal by reference to which the
artist represents those objects which do not themselves
appear to the eye, so with our minds we conceive the ideal
of perfect eloquence, but with our ears we catch only the
copy.[17]

In sculpture, painting, or a description of the perfect
orator, the result is not something unrelated to nature
but rather a composite drawn according to an extension
of natural particulars into a whole that not only sur-
passes any particular human or natural object, but also
whose form has an entirely different reference. From the
point of view of the spectator of art, its material form, or
species, leads the mind to contemplate the ideal the
artist has labored to embody. One of the most interesting things about Cicero's theory is his point that even a
statue by Phidias, which is born not from copying a
model but from an imagined perfection, still falls short of
the degree of perfection the human mind can conceive.
If we accept this point, we are bound to conclude that
the spectator of a painting or the reader of a poem sees
an approximation of perfection from which he can
imagine something still better. Thus Fracastoro's notion
that the features of a statue or painting incarnate "the
simple idea clothed in its own beauties" should perhaps
be understood to refer to a kind of proximate representation. Perfection lies not only beyond the particulars of
nature but also beyond, though not so far beyond, the
imagery of art; from an epistemological point of view it is
articulated only in the mind of the artist and his audience.

In *Turrius* Fracastoro says that there are two ways in

which the soul responds to those things it perceives or knows, by sensitive appetite and by will, and in moving on to this stage of the discussion, we enter the territory of the moral significance of literature. The mind inevitably approaches a point at which it decides whether what it perceives is good or evil: "If therefore the soul is offered something good by the senses, its intention is called appetite; if it is offered good through the intellect, its intention is called will."[18] We can now begin to understand the motive for Fracastoro's insistence upon the necessity of the poetic fiction, for what the poet invents or "adds to the subject" is really designed to enter the mind of the reader as a "phantasm," moving through its faculties just as a reconstituted image of a "universal" takes it journey from "subnotion" through imagination, phantasy, judgment, and intellect to the will. In one sense Fracastoro's account of fiction makes it an abstraction, for it derives from the mode of perfected idea both he and Cicero discuss. But this fiction is by no means disembodied, any more than in its own medium a statue by Phidias is disembodied. The ordering and deliberating powers of the mind are still at work upon images that have a material appearance. If one refers these images to truth of fact, then they are lies; if one refers them to conceptual truth, they fiction in the most important way, as Boccaccio and Sidney insist. It is clear once again that the validity of such art relies on the reader to understand the relationship of the image to fact on the one hand and concept on the other.

But there is also a somewhat different sense in which the relationship between image and idea should concern us. Fracastoro gets at this by answering the objections of one of the speakers in *Naugerius*, Bardulone, who re-

marks that what the poet "adds" to truth are "extrane-
ous accessories, which I see are called fiction by some."[19]
The response is to suggest an almost organic integrity to
the fusion of concept and expression. I say "almost"
because Fracastoro's argument is not that such a fusion
is necessary to truth as truth, but that its reception and
its ability to affect the minds of the audience demands all
the equipment the artist brings to the execution of his
task.

> For if you mean whatever is added to the bare object, cer-
> tainly it will be enough to use ordinary speech in explaining
> things, for other refinements are not necessary. . . . But,
> indeed, if we consider objects as they should be, and look
> for perfection, these additions will not only not be extrane-
> ous but essential. . . . Do you not see that just as perfection
> and ornament are a real part of the things which nature
> produces, so they are of the things which art produces?
> What perfection and beauty are, only the great artists know.
> And if you take them away from the subject, assuredly you
> have somehow taken away life itself. Therefore what the
> painters and poets add to things for perfection is not ex-
> traneous, if we mean by "thing" not the bare object such as
> common artificers, or those who are controlled and re-
> stricted by some purpose, make, but the object perfected
> and given life. Then, if what is added *makes manifest* the
> perfection and excellence of the subject, ought we not to
> concede one and for all its great usefulness and desirability?[20]

Yet this may beg the question. Can the poet fashion
perfection perfectly? According to Dante the beauty of
divine truth was such that its true form lay beyond the
powers of human vision. Even imploring divine aid the
poet could only approximately convey what had been

revealed to him. Allowing for Fracastoro's somewhat
less exalted view of the immaterial, we can nevertheless
see that his confidence in the poet's vision is somewhat
greater. He seems close to suggesting that only the poet
can exhibit the idea as it really is, that fiction and style
bring out its true beauty as cutting and polishing beauti-
fy the otherwise hidden luster of a precious stone. And
Bardulone his interlocutor is dissatisfied precisely because what seems to elicit perfection is fictitious and
therefore untrue. The implication is that perfection itself
might be a lie. "Everything, then," he complains, "is
partly untrue and partly invented and exaggerated. You
have just said rightly that poets portray many things that
do not exist in reality. That they present open and
shameless falsehoods can be seen in what Virgil writes
of Aeneas and Dido, who, it is known, lived in widely
separated periods. Since all these things are false, truly I
do not see how they can be beautiful, for everything
false is ugly, since it consists of things that are not
real."[21]

Interestingly Fracastoro's response is not to refer once
again to the ideal and to insist on its validity, but to
respond in a somewhat more diffuse statement that
"everything which may be allowed to invention is true,
either because it has the appearance of truth, or because
it has allegorical significance, or because it accords with
the universal, the simply beautiful idea, and not with the
particular."[22] This doesn't really answer Bardulone's
question; it simply reasserts propositions already made.
And Fracastoro's case finally rests, not on any proof of
the superior truth of the universal idea, but on the poet's
ability to produce an effect of deep intensity. He has
Naugerius say that as a reader "I shall not only love, but

be struck with wonder, and I shall feel that a divine something has entered my soul," and he adds, somewhat anticlimactically, "If men wish to know about agriculture, natural science, philosophy, and any other subjects that the poet has written about, they will go to the poet, not those who wish to know the bare and in a way rude facts, but those who desire to see objects, as it were, alive, perfected and adorned with their own appropriate beauties."[23]

As Weinberg remarks, "This is a very curious work in the series of poetic arts. . . . It is concerned almost entirely with the ends of poetry, with seeking definition and redefinition as the concept of the ends is progressively refined."[24] This is so, but if we take Fracastoro's phrase "perfected and adorned" to mean that the poet's task is merely the ornamentation of all knowledge, to make him as Weinberg implies, merely a rhetorician, then we miss the point. For perfection and adornment are, as his dialogues on thinking and on the soul tell us, essential to our accurate and convinced knowledge of things. These are the qualities that bring the ideal alive into the mind in terms that would help men to agree on truth. These propositions cater to the reader's need to experience ideas, which they can only do through the images of materiality reshaped into the universals latent in them.

BARBARO

Fracastoro was not alone in facing these issues. Daniele Barbaro, whose theory will conclude this chapter, and Sir Philip Sidney, the subject of the next, are also occupied with mediating concept and image as they explore the validity and affective function of art. And Barbaro gives a good deal of attention to one issue ignored by Fracastoro: the tendency of the human mind to err.

Barbaro's *Della Eloquenza* (1557)[25] is a rambling, rather bizarre colloquy involving the voices and views of Nature, Art, and Soul (a fourth figure, Dinardo—*Dio/ Natura/Arte*—appears near the end), concluding with an exposition of the techniques of oratory. The treatise is not a poetics, but its central concerns are sufficiently close to the didactic theories we are involved with to make it of interest. Barbaro is primarily dealing with the artful structuring of words: the pivotal abstraction Art can be defined as the mind's effort to accommodate truth to the soul by verbally refashioning the images of nature.

The motive for such a refashioning turns on the belief that the two "counselors" of the soul, intellect and appetite, are inclined to move in different directions (p. 347). A lengthy explanation of the appetites suggests that without guidance they tend to fasten on the immediate experience of the senses from which gratification or repulsion are derived. This process is disorderly, even chaotic, yet by their motion and persuasion the entire being is allowed to function. Barbaro has previously indicated the condition of the soul in a fallen world: it attends to appearances or fables, for although nature provides through the senses the means by which reason can operate, the soul is lost without art (p. 346). From this point on, Art proceeds to explain how this is so.

First of all, the general problem is to adjust words to things, that is, to the truth. Part of the solution lies in the soul's natural inner harmony—a potential harmony effected only when reason rules the appetites (pp. 346–348). The intellect or reason is moved by proofs and reasons (opinion is a kind of weak and uncertain version of reason), but appetite is moved by the senses and imagination. The soul may be confused if subjected to too great a variety of movements, but art can bring order and direction by use of memory and imagination (pp. 349–352). The imagination, Art says, is the power that "puts things before our eyes" (p. 352). Soul objects that it can be confused or even build castles in the air or construct insane visions, Art answers,

> "However vainly that power may be used, so much the more ought it to be used and employed in a greater service. By means of it a man first decides what he wishes others to be; then he decides within himself in the best and most excellent way he can those things which he seeks to present to the understanding of others. . . . A like power is evident in painting, whose artifice is that the painter depicts each form which he seeks to have appear on his canvas firmly in his imagination; and the more his imagination is fine and vigorous, the more illustrious and praised is his painting. The forms and semblances of anger are many, but one especially expresses the irascible power. That one ought much more than the others to touch the phantasy, and by that the paintbrush and the tongue should be directed. And thus everything is done in the most effective way either for moving or delighting or instructing in order to reach him who reasons, so that he may listen as he wishes." (Pp. 352–353)

Thus the positive value of imagination is twofold. In the mind of the artist it is the power to invent forms—images of the abstraction the artist has in mind. (Barbaro's concept is very much the same as Sidney's notion of the poet's "fore-conceit," which will be discussed in the next chapter.) The listener or reader, like the spectator of a painting, is touched affectively and rationally, and Barbaro goes on to explain this process at length. Essentially his argument is that the mind is best prepared to reason when it is in a state of more or less calm delight, a state in which the images present to the imagination are exactly suited to our common perceptive powers.

At the same time Barbaro is especially alert to the vagaries of imagining. He points out that human appetites (irascible and concupiscible) are subject to moderation and excess and that these modes of appetite are partially dependent upon the manner in which objects of desire and aversion are presented (pp. 354–356). Affections may in part be directed by "the sweet harmony of eloquence," and since the rules of art are uniform and unchanging, those who observe them are able to dominate the minds of others (pp. 358–359).

The inferences to be drawn from Art's presentation thus far are these: the human will, responding to and directing appetite tends to determine what objects will be embraced or avoided, but this natural and partially random process can be influenced and modified by art, which chooses those images to be offered to the mind and presents them in such a way as to make them appealing or distasteful. But Nature objects that this process is complicated by the nature of things and by the tendency of the receiving imagination to respond individually or diversely. In other words, the discernment of truth is made difficult both by the nature of the object and the weakness of the perceiving mind:

> I say, then, that a thing is either manifest and clear in itself, or in no way possesses light and splendor; but illuminated

by that which does possess light, it becomes open to the human senses. In the first category is the sun and all the bodies which are called luminous. In the second are colored bodies which in themselves do not have the brilliance of clarity, but are illuminated by something else. The same is found in the intellect, which, receiving anything quickly, apprehends and retains that, after which it has that light within it. And if I were to invent names, I would call these "notions" or really "first intentions." But when there are other things which do not have light in themselves or any vividness, and therefore a judgment is made about them with the suspicion that their illumination comes from another place than their own intelligence. From this is derived opinion, which, since it is opinion, is neither true nor false. The defect derives from that power which we spoke of a little before [imagination]. For to me things are as they are, but being received into the soul, by some weak semblance they are carried from the senses into the phantasy and become oddly mixed, producing diverse opinions. Yet it is certainly true that I do not make one thing so different from another that man is unable to find some similarity between them. (P. 360)

Nature adds that the capacity to discover resemblances frequently results in error and that whatever has the appearance of natural fact remains so fixed in the mind "that very often the lie finds a place in it more than truth." Error may consist in mistaking the sense in which something is true or in assigning the wrong causes to things. These occur "when reason inclines more to the senses than to the intellect and more to appearance than to essence" (p. 361). Anything, such as art, which employs appearances or resemblances is in danger of being misunderstood or misused. Thus the ancient problem that proximity to the experience of the senses places art in the realm of epistemological error resurfaces here, and because Barbaro places such great emphasis on the role of the affections, the moral issue, the possibility that the will may choose the wrong object, adds to the difficulty he attempts to confront.

At this stage of the discussion Soul concludes that because man is drawn to appearances more than to essences, it is better that he not inquire into the causes of things, but Art replies that the mind must deal with resemblances because that is the only route to knowledge (pp. 364–365). The following passage is Barbaro's effort to settle the issue.

Soul: It is necessary then to pay more attention to resemblance than to truth?

Art: It is necessary; and since you do it by no other thing, you and anyone else who seeks to persuade others are obliged to do it thus, in order that it may be both heard and understood by the people, who quite often pay attention to a lie because in it there is some aspect of the truth. . . .

Soul: Tell me, please, when men give their belief to something which appears true, do they not do it because the truth pleases them?

Art: Yes.

Soul: Can something unknown ever be pleasing?

Art: No, never.

Soul: It is necessary, then, that truth should be known by men?

Art: It is necessary.

Soul: Why, then, do they embrace the appearance more than the truth?

Art: Because they think that the semblance is the truth itself.

Soul: Therefore, they do not have a knowledge of the truth.

Art: Don't you deceive yourself also, O Soul. Because natural understanding of the truth is quite weak and confused, like a woman who, submitting to the senses, leaves reason and intellect aside. And if no one knows it or can render testimony, she is one of those who from the first beginning of mortal existence to the last extreme of their lives, unmoved by doctrine or any practise, resigns her judgment to sentiments or to those forces which are closest to her. Those sentiments, leading reason away from her, make false and inconstant guides; but if opinion is bound to reason in such a way that it cannot escape, then what will gracefully emerge from its being will no longer be called opinion but knowledge. (P. 365)

The appeal to reason seems especially weak at this point, and Art acknowledges that not everyone has the same sense of the verisimilar. Those without learning, or idiots, perceive it quite differently from the educated. So Art must go on to explain the verisimilar in more detail. Traces or vestiges of resemblances occur in the superficialities of things perceived by the senses before any rational inquiry has occurred. From these results the verisimilar, which appears the same to everyone. Only when reason begins to operate analytically and dominantly on these perceptions do differences appear. If the appetites are uncorrected by rational deliberation, then no proper distinctions can be made, especially those that discriminate the material from the intellectual. Art says, "And again I tell you and affirm that everyone confusedly apprehends and desires a good in what seems to pacify the soul. But then, carried away by the appetites (as the intellect is first carried away by the phantasy) and turning to them, he mistakes the true path of that good by which each one, moved by the power of Nature, struggles to reach it" (p. 368).

One of the consequences of this view is the promotion of a kind of verisimilitude, an effort to favor images that have a likeness to the truths sought by the intellect. There is some difference here from the position of Fracastoro, who, as we have seen, is more confident in the human power to recognize the lie in fiction as it discovers the truth behind it. Barbaro reflects, in part, a growing tendency in sixteenth-century theory to urge upon art as great a verisimilitude as possible. This much is implicit in remarks that accompany a discussion of the nature of pleasure and pain. Art says that

> those things are gratifying and pleasing which conform to nature. . . . And since for each individual what is gratifying is that to which by nature he is inclined, so for the same reason a sweet and pleasant thing is that which is customary, as what is most suited to nature. . . . Learning is also a pleasant thing, for the imitation of things is most delightful, because the power and contrast of art, not the things expressed, habitually delight. Whence it is that pictures, statues, and feigned works please those who contemplate them. (P. 373)

Conformity to nature, however, is the achievement of art, and this is declared most emphatically in a passage some pages on in the context of Art's explanation of language. The passage opens with the general assertion that the force and virtue of language are marvelous:

> Because besides the intention of the conceits and wishes of you mortals, which it alone makes public with universal and

open delight, there is no feeling from any appetite in you
which is not fiercely excited and moved by it. And if anyone
wishes to enter into argument about this, he will find that,
every time he comes to consider the way in which [speech]
is used among you, things in the senses are of less power in
moving the senses than speech, whenever it is formed and
constructed in a lovely, effective, skilful way; and then,
after more profound consideration, he will know that the
value of speech itself is almost infinite, since it alone shows
the substance and causes of things to the intellect. (P. 380)

Like Fracastoro, Barbaro concentrates on the manner of
presentation. Both maintain that it is what the artist does
with images which distinguishes them from the confusing stream of particular sense experiences and gives
them some degree of conceptual clarity, and this is
necessary if language is to elicit the natural power of the
mind to understand universal truth.

However, Barbaro develops a far more acute sense of
the weakness of the natural powers. It is a moral and
intellectual weakness, traceable to the imagination when
it is free to influence the appetites and the intellect in
random and unschooled ways. For Barbaro the human
appetites are powerful. They constitute our habitual
response to daily and particular experience and prey
upon the natural instinct to turn to the good and avoid
the evil. If the soul were able to function by intellect
alone, there would be little problem. It would be in
direct contact with eternal truth, with the tranquil and
settled order of things. But appetite can overwhelm and
govern the intellect, inhibiting its power to judge with
accuracy and penetration, and this is where, for Barbaro,
the verbal arts come in. Language is primarily the mind's
capacity to record things truly, but it is also a powerful

affective instrument, more powerful than sense experience. If the two capacities are joined so that the affective force of language is expressed in images that are similitudes of true things, then the soul of the auditor or reader may well be moved to cling feelingly to true judgment and opinion. Barbaro's argument, like that of Sidney which we will examine in the next chapter, proposes that the artist appeals to the intellect through the very faculties that without the assistance of art may be its enemies.

IV

"The Gates of Popular Judgments": Sidney's Apology for Poetry (Ca. 1581–1583)

The phrase that heads this chapter is taken from a passage early in the *Apology* in which Sidney begins to argue both the superiority and the priority of imaginative literature over philosophy and history. It is a statement typical of Sidney's pronounced tendency to judge all disciplines, not just poetry, by their reference to an audience. In broad terms they all have an identical goal, the reformation of the will and the improvement of behavior. *Praxis* is a more important end than *gnosis*. On these terms poetry can lay claim to the dignity of learned discourse, and much more: "So that the ending end of all earthly learning being virtuous action, those skills, that most serve to bring forth that, have a most just title to be princes over all the rest."[1] To vindicate the poet's skills is apparently the major theme of the *Apology*, since poetry is not unique in its aims, only in its means. Like all forms of learning it is instrumental, but its instruments are, Sidney argues, more telling and more certain. In contrast to a good deal of Italian criticism (to which he was frequently indebted) Sidney does not isolate the poet's role as imitator as his defining trait, nor does he argue that the usefulness of his art is a by-product or accident of that substantial and central purpose.[2] Instead the influence of Sidney's didactic bias stems from his view of the nature of the reader's mind: overtly or by implication his criticism refers almost constantly to theories of normative mental responses, in particular those elicited, according to his inherited Humanism, by the arts of persuasion. We should begin then by noticing his reference to the senses, mainly sight and to a lesser degree hearing.

The series of excerpts which follows dwells on the point that real knowledge involves familiarity. From his early remarks that poetry was the "first light-giver to ignorance" (96. 12) to his concluding mock-invective against those "who cannot hear the planet-like music" or who possess "so earth-creeping a mind that it cannot lift itself up to look at the sky of Poetry" (142. 20–22), Sidney concentrates on the power of the poet and his art virtually to compel an immediate and practical understanding, even as he urges the elevated value of the art and its moral consequences. The "notable Prosopopeias" of the Psalmist "maketh you, as it were, see God coming in His majesty" (99. 16–17). The poet's intrusion is a kind of gift: "Having no law but wit," he "bestow[s] that in colours upon you which is fittest for the eye to see" (102. 28–30). There is even a humorous illustration of the visual in a caricature of moral philosophers "whom me thinketh, I see coming towards me with a sullen gravity, as though they could not abide vice by daylight, rudely clothed for to witness outwardly their contempt for outward things, with books in their hands against glory . . ." (105. 1–5). And, "See whether wisdom and temperance in Ulysses and Diomedes, valour in Achilles, friendship in Nisus and Euryalus, even to an ignorant man carry not an apparent shining . . . and finally, all virtues, vices, and passions so in their own natural seats laid to view, that we seem not to hear of them, but clearly to see through them" (109. 6–9, 15–18). To abolish distance and detachment the poet "will show you in Tantalus, Atreus, and such like, nothing that is not to be shunned; in Cyrus, Aeneas, Ulysses, each thing to be followed . . ." (110.10–12). Even evil men will "steal to see the form of goodness (which seen they cannot but love) ere themselves be aware, as if they took a medecine of cherries" (114. 30–32). Nathan caused David "as in a glass to see his own filthiness, as that heavenly psalm of mercy well testifieth" (115. 24–26), and comedy, "an imitation of the common errors of our life," leads the beholder to see the "filthiness of evil" as a foil "to perceive the beauty of virtue" (117. 11–18). Finally, the "heroicall" poet, "who maketh magnanimity and justice shine through all misty fearfulness and foggy desires; who, if the saying of Plato and Tully be true, that who could see virtue would be wonderfully ravished with the love of her beauty—this man sets her out to make her more lovely in her holiday apparel, to the eye of any that will deign not to disdain until they understand" (119. 18–24).

As Sidney evokes the sensory in these phrases, it is the necessary starting point on the road to knowledge.

This is a belief common to Humanist concepts of education and firmly established in rhetorical theory.[3] There is also Aristotle's old brief that images are the content of thought, and for Sidney the terms of visual experience are the governing model for the language necessary to convey complicated modes of responsive thought. He supposes that knowledge occurs in a fashion analogous to viewing a scene or a picture, and it should be understood that his use of the concept of *ut pictura poesis* is more than simply conventional or convenient: it reveals something utterly fundamental about his view of cognition. He is arguing that the visualisable images of literature are as close as language can come to recreating the clarity of the ordinary experience of the senses. It is this sort of experience we find most certain, reassuring, and compelling. Our knowledge of moral values, then, must begin in something close to our knowledge of material objects, and as the next example suggests, Sidney has a most un-Platonic confidence that we can know what we see.

> For as in outward things, to a man that had never seen an elephant or a rhinoceros, who would tell him most exquisitely all their shapes, colour, bigness, and particular marks; or of a gorgeous palace, the architecture, with declaring the full beauties might well make the hearer able to repeat, as it were by rote, all he had heard, yet should never satisfy his inward conceits with being witness to itself of a true lively knowledge; but the same man as soon as he might see those beasts well painted, or the house well in model, should straightways grow, without need of any description, to a judicial comprehending of them: so no doubt the philosopher with his learned definition—be it of virtue, vices, matters of public policy or private government—

> replenisheth the memory with many infallible grounds of
> wisdom, which, notwithstanding, lie dark before the imagi-
> native and judging power, if they be not illuminated or
> figured forth by the speaking picture of poetry. (107. 18—34)

It might be argued that knowledge of the lineaments of a rhinoceros is easier to come by than a grasp of moral conditions. But the operable distinction is not between actual and imaginative seeing, but between modes of presenting what cannot be directly experienced. Language closest to the pictorial will ensure the most direct, accurate, and lasting comprehension. The reader's imaginative power is that part of his mind able to receive presentations, to be illuminated, as it were. We may note in passing that Sidney's position is different from that of Augustine, who argued that an innate idea of a perfect form of any object permitted us to judge the quality of a particular example. For Sidney it is the model that is to be judged and which is supplied from without by the painterly poet. This assistance is necessary because unaided we cannot "see" our own moral condition. Hence the usefulness of comedy: ". . . there is no man living but by the force truth hath in Nature, no sooner seeth these men play their parts, but wisheth them *in pistrinum*; although perchance the sack of his own faults lie so behind his back that he seeth not himself dance to the same measure; whereto yet nothing can more open his eyes than to find his own actions contemptibly set forth" (117. 26—32).

But vivid or lively or accurate presentation is not in itself sufficient for moral education, which is for Sidney much more than an illustrated lecture. Poetic images must also be able to stir the affections and appetites.

Most of the statements already examined contain language indicating that recognition and some kind of emotive response accompany each other and that in some cases the response is virtually automatic: even evil men will "steal to see the form of goodness (which seen they cannot but love) ere themselves be aware" (114. 30–32). However, the issue is not really that simple, for here Sidney is conflating a part of conventional affective theory which elsewhere in the *Apology* receives more extended, if not exactly systematic, treatment.

A major premise in the argument against philosophy is that, whatever the truths it is capable of professing, it is unlikely to reach an audience. The philosopher's disadvantage in the marketplace of education is considerable:

> For his knowledge standeth so upon the abstract and general, that happy is that man who may understand him, and more happy that can apply what he doth understand. . . .
>
> The Philosopher showeth you the way, he informeth you of the particularities, as well as of the tediousness of the way, as of the pleasant lodging you shall have when your journey is ended, as of the many by-turnings that may divert you from your way. But this is to no man but to him that will read him, and read him with attentive studious painfulness; which constant desire whosoever hath in him hath already passed half the hardness of the way, and therefore is beholding to the philosopher but for the other half. (107. 1–4, 112. 39–113. 8)

The reader Sidney has in mind has not, in effect, even begun the journey, and he has little taste for intellectual difficulty or for the prospect of arduous moral struggle.

He is clearly a common reader—the category into which most of us fit—and must be led by his inclination to pleasure to give his attention to those manifestations of virtue and vice most likely to encourage the practice of a redemptive morality. That the natural animal impulse to pleasure might be an avenue to knowledge is an ancient commonplace,[4] and Sidney's sweeping assertions that there are elements in art which entice the reader to continuing attention would serve only to place him rather obviously in the large context of Horatian and rhetorical criticism if he had offered a less sustained account of the whole question. In effect what the *Apology* does is to break the topic down into some of its elements: First, does pleasure precede or follow knowledge? Second, what features of a poem or of a work of art in general are the occasions for pleasurable response? Third, are the pleasures derived from art sensory or imaginative or in some way rational?

1.

Sidney's understanding of the sequence of affect may be confusing, partly because he talks at times as if all response occurred simultaneously. But most classical and later accounts of pleasure or pain maintain that some degree of knowledge of an object must occur before the mind "judges" it, that is classifies it as something to be accepted or avoided. By themselves the senses react only on the level of sensation (though a kind of rudimentary pleasure or pain attends them); it is the internal senses that enable us to identify objects, and these, as we have seen, are primarily associated with sight, which allows us to register objects at a distance.

Since pleasure and distress are first of all general classi-
fications for sorting out all responses of the sensitive
soul to objects seen or heard or recalled in the imagination, and since pleasure and pain are "passions" (that is,
reactions of the organism which may lead to some form
of action), it was argued that no affective response
beyond the most rudimentary sensation could precede
cognition.[5]

In the light of this basic proposition it may appear that
the first sonnet of *Astrophil and Stella*, which summarizes
a theory of the stages of poetic affect, proposes a reverse
order:

> Loving in truth, and faine in verse my love to show,
> That the deare She might take some pleasure of my paine:
> Pleasure might cause her reade, reading might make
>   her know. . . .[6]

How can Stella experience pleasure before knowledge?
The answer is, I think, implicit in the second line: she
would at the very least have to identify Astrophil's pain
before she could take delight in its representation.
Further reading would then yield knowledge of the
cause of suffering (herself), and by this chain of reaction,
so Astrophil's theory goes, she might be moved to pity
and thence to action ("and pity grace obtain"). This way
of reading the poem, though it ignores for the moment
that what is in question is a predicted response to art
rather than to something directly experienced, is at least
consistent with what Sidney writes in the *Apology*.[7] An
initial affective response follows a kind of rough cognition, and is in fact nearly coincident with it. A major
statement in the *Apology* attempts to spell out the man-

ner in which poetry should begin to solicit our minds:

> Now therein of all sciences (I speak still of human, and according to human conceits) is our poet the monarch. For he doth not only show the way, but giveth so sweet a prospect into the way, as will entice any man to enter into it. Nay, he doth, as if your journey should lie through a fair vineyard, at the first give you a cluster of grapes, that full of that taste, you may long to pass further. He beginneth not with obscure definitions, which must blur the margent with interpretations, and load the memory with doubtfulness; but he cometh to you with words set in delightful proportion, either accompanied with, or prepared for the well enchanting skill of music, with a tale forsooth he cometh unto you, with a tale which holdeth children from play, and old men from the chimney corner. (113. 18-31)

It is clear enough from this account that imagery and language directed at sensory pleasure accompany, if they do not actually precede, the gradual unfolding of meaning. The poet's initial appeal is to modes of elementary pleasure, to the childish in man, and this is deliberate, not casual.

2.

It is not sufficient to ground a theory of literary affect on general and natural responses to sensory images, but Sidney's theory certainly begins in proposing a close parallel between our reactions to the natural and the artistic. Similar, perhaps identical, modes of appetite and perception are supposed to describe the orientation of the self to both kinds of object. Yet Sidney needs to account for the superiority of art over random nature, for he has begun the essay by trumpeting poetry as a mode of learning preeminent for the skills it demands of the artist. Moreover, we can expect some explanation of his reliance on Aristotle's observation that even painful events are made attractive by the medium of imitation.[8]

Sixteenth-century Italian critics offer a variety of explanations for what it is in literature that delights us: ornament or mode of treatment; the verisimilar; a mixture of truth and falsehood in the story; or some possibility of relating fictional events to the reader's own situation. In different parts of his commentary on the *Poetics* Castelvetro mentions nearly all these.[9] Scaliger, one of Sidney's sources, remarks that our delight in art comes from perceiving the grace in things; it is a satisfaction produced by imagined perfection, harmony, and order.[10] But this is rather too general if we wish to know which elements in art are designed to exhibit such qualities. As for Sidney, we may look first of all at the description of Kalander's garden near the beginning of the *New Arcadia* for an account of visual art in terms of its impact upon the spectator:

> . . . for as soone as the descending of the stayres had delivered them downe, they came into a place cunninglie set with trees of the moste tast-pleasing fruites, but scarcelie they had taken that into their consideration, but that they were suddainely stept into a delicate greene, of each side of the greene a thicket bend, behinde the thickets againe new beddes of flowers, which being under the trees, the trees were to them a Pavilion, and they to the trees a mosaical floore: so that it seemed that arte therein would needes be delightfull by counterfaiting his enemie error, and making order in confusion.
>
> In the middest of all the place, was a faire ponde, whose

> shaking christall was a perfect mirrour to all the other
> beauties, so that it bare shewe of two gardens; one in deede,
> the other in shaddowes: and in one of the thickets was a fine
> fountaine made thus. A naked *Venus* of white marble,
> wherein the graver had used such cunning, that the naturall
> blew veines of the marble were framed in fitte places, to
> sett foorth the beautiful veines of her bodie.[11]

The pleasure the garden evokes in the fictional spectators is sensory at base but its real force lies in their perception of the artist's skill at mimetic illusion, a power to
approximate the random and the natural while suggesting that everything is calculated and orderly. Order
governs the arrangement of individual items and also
their sequence, so that the viewer is led from landscape
to human figures, at first mythological, and later characters in the fiction introduced by their portraits (if we
read beyond this quotation). One necessary condition of
this process is that the spectator be sharply reminded of
the lifelikeness of the artificial and at the same time quite
certain that it is artificial. But similarity and difference
are so closely bound up with each other that we are
teased into delight at the artist's skill at managing these
effects. Our pleasure, he implies, is in imitation, but the
most important aspect of imitation is in the vividness or
liveliness of the image created by the artist. Though
Sidney never quite says so, this mode of pleasure may
well be what serves to block out a reaction of distress at
the representation of pain or suffering.

In the *Apology* Sidney attributes pleasure variously to
choice and arrangement of words and to meter (113.
27–29), to the visual properties of an idealized landscape (100. 29–33), to artistic imitation generally (102.
34), and to the tale or narrative (113. 30). No single

property of literary art is exclusively responsible, but at the same time all these causes are the artist's doing. So, while the affective capacities they work upon are natural, the causes are to be found in artifice, and by rejecting the concept of divine furor (130. 7–10) Sidney avoids any suggestion that cause and effect may be uncalculated. What is both invented and vivid is thus central to his defensive strategy.

This is nowhere more evident than in the section of the *Apology* where he seeks to refute "the most important imputations laid to the poor poets" (123. 1–2). The first charge is that "there being many other more fruitful knowledges, a man might better spend his time in them than in this" (123. 3–4). I shall deal with his answer a bit later. The second charge, that poetry "is the mother of lies" (123. 5), is partly countered in the statement that the poet "nothing affirms, and therefore never lieth" (123. 38–39) and also in Sidney's judgment that we do not take representation literally (124. 17–19). I shall also return to this issue. The third objection, that poetry "is the nurse of abuse, infecting us with many pestilent desires, with a siren's sweetness drawing the mind to the serpent's tale of sinful fancy . . ." (123. 5–8) is less easy to deal with, since it might well turn Sidney's insistence on the affective capacities of literature against him. Indeed he has to make some major concessions:

> For I will not deny but that man's wit may make Poesy, which should be *eikastike*, which some learned have defined, 'figuring forth good things', to be *phantastike*, which doth contrariwise infect the fancy with unworthy objects;[12] . . . Nay truly, though I yield that Poesy may not only be abused, but that being abused, by reason of his sweet charming force, it can do more hurt than any other army of

words, yet shall it be so far from concluding that the abuse should give reproach to the abused, that contrariwise it is a good reason, that whatsoever, being abused, doth most harm, being rightly used (and upon the right use each thing conceiveth his title), doth most good. (125. 25–26, 35–39; 126. 1–3)

In other words the affective power is neutral; it derives from the poet's means, his technique or mode of representing, and may be used for good or ill. Up to a point this seems a sufficient reply to one kind of objection.

Yet we may wonder if Sidney really considers fiction morally neutral. He has argued that it raises the poet above the level of the historian (who has "been glad to borrow fashion and perchance weight of poets" [97. 22–24]) and sets him apart from the philosopher (whose arguments are abstract and therefore lacking in attraction). We may remember that Sidney begins the *Apology* by dignifying poetry as a superior form of learning. And if fiction does not really lie, at least circumstantially, it cannot be the object of responsible objection. Yet it is nevertheless a major source of the appeal and effectiveness of literature, and Sidney argues repeatedly that "fruitfulness" is the central reason for preferring poetry above all other modes of discourse. From one angle, the poetic lie is not harmful because no one accepts it as true;[13] from another angle, it and all the trappings of poetic technique in which it is clothed are absolutely essential.

Sidney's way out of these difficulties amounts to much more than piecemeal replies to objections broken down into their categories. He requires that the poet hold to morally acceptable doctrine, but this is not where the real force of his argument lies, since doctrine verges on irrelevance if it cannot be used to redeem.

First of all, he expects of the reader or spectator a complex imaginative response. In part that response involves Aristotle's belief that imagined events do not affect us in quite the same way as actual events.[14] In other words, what our imagination accepts as an artistic representation we understand as both real and unreal. We understand a mode of representation to be just that, but we attend to meaning in a different way. As in the description of Kalander's garden, one part of the mind knows that the artificial is only a mimicry of the living. Yet at the same time the mimicry is sufficiently close so that the difference is not too radical. If we return for a moment to the statue of Venus and Aeneas, we can discover what Sidney is up to. As we have seen, he first notes how the sculptor has used the veins in the marble to approximate the veins in the human body. What the statuary depicts is the infant Aeneas ignoring his mother's flowing breast and smiling up into her eyes, and this level of the work of art yields quite another kind of significance. Yet here as well we have imagery, not disembodied meaning. But the object of imitation is clearly an idea incarnate in certain visual properties of the worked marble. The spectator understands at once that the whole is a piece of fiction and yet a truth he can believe. As Sidney points out in the *Apology*, the poet's "delivering forth also is not wholly imaginative, as we are wont to say by them that build castles in the air . . ." (107. 7−8). The poet, like the sculptor, is not content to feign just the circumstantial apparatus of his work or merely to create his style, he also makes "notable images of virtues, vices, or what else . . ." (103. 29). These especially must be seen by the reader and attract him by their ideal character. It is at this level of art that Sidney finds "the universal consideration," the poet's other nature, the golden world of what ought to be and may be. Having entered this world, the reader must then be moved by its images toward some approximation in his own behavior.

3.

In order to understand what Sidney means by "moving," we must first realize that delight and moving are not exactly the same thing, even though they are closely related and even though Sidney's language often makes them appear to be identical in his mind. The difference is obvious in Sonnet 1 of *Astrophil and Stella*: it is intended that Stella first of all take pleasure in the manner in which Astrophil's pain is represented. He then means her to be moved to pity and to "grace," so that we have, in theory, distinct stages of affect: delight, knowledge, sympathetic emotion, and willed action. When Sidney remarks in the *Apology* that the old ballad of Percy and Douglas moves his heart "more than with a trumpet" (118. 26), and wonders what the effect would be had it been composed in the eloquence of Pindar, the example concentrates on the strength of feeling even simple poetry can command, but it clearly includes the effects of style as party to the aim of producing emotion. Delight is both a general prelude to and an accompaniment of modes of feeling more precise and focused and based in part upon the knowledge delight has prompted one to refine. Above all we need to remember that delight, for Sidney, is bound up in the near-sensory, imaginal properties of art.

To sum up the discussion thus far, pleasure both precedes and follows knowledge because Sidney appears to break knowledge down into a kind of preliminary cognition succeeded by more complete understanding; the work of art as a whole occasions pleasure, but its main source is in the fusion of a kind of fiction with a kind of truth; and finally, delight must be distinguished from specific emotions that are rational at least in the sense that they are to be commanded to morally proper ends.

Had Sidney been more careful or systematic with his terms—had he, for example, always distinguished delight from moving—he would I think have come close to a mechanical theory of affect, a theory that would relate different features of art too nicely to separate faculties in the reader. But his emphasis tends towards the continuous, even intensified, preservation of emotive response. This is evident in his celebration of heroic poetry, "which is not only a kind, but the best and most accomplished kind of poetry. For as the image of each action stirreth and instructeth the mind, so the lofty image of such worthies most inflameth the mind with desire to be worthy" (119. 26–30). The statement postulates an increasing intensity of feeling, but interestingly enough the mind is meant to respond first to individual actions and then to character. Moreover, stirring seems to be more or less passive, while inflaming implies an active desire to emulate a model, and this is a movement or appetite of the will.

Sidney's convictions in these matters also demand that connections between levels of affect must be governed by the worthiness of the image, that is by its emodiment of universal principle, and what he means

by universals needs now to be looked at somewhat more
closely. In one sense universals refer to accepted and
recognized doctrines for moral behavior, which Sidney
suggests are inherited from the moral philosopher.[15] He
in turn "standeth upon the natural virtues, vices, and
passions of men . . ." (100. 8). But if universals derive
from nature, they are in a most important sense above
and beyond it. Perhaps the most familiar of Sidney's
statements in this regard is his peroration to the early
paragraphs of the *Apology* where he celebrates the poet's
exclusive capacity to conceive a better world: "Only the
poet, disdaining to be tied to any such subjection, lifted
up with the vigor of his own invention, doth grow in
effect into another nature, in making things either better
than Nature bringeth forth, or, quite anew, forms such
as never were in Nature . . ." (100. 21–25). Later he
restates his concept of what the poet fashions as "what
should or should not be" (124. 9) and in another place
quotes Chapter 9 of the *Poetics* to the effect that poetry is
more philosophical than history because it "dealeth with
katholou, that is to say, with the universal consideration"
(109. 26–27). On the basis of such statements as these it
has seemed proper to some interpreters of Sidney to
argue that he thinks of the poet as conceiving an ideal
that is initially devoid of material content, and that it is
just such a naked abstraction the reader must eventually
hold in his mind. If we accept this version of his
thought, there is ample warrant for marking him as a
Platonist or Neoplatonist and for identifying his theory
of poetic creation as something akin to the standard view
of the way medieval allegory comes about. Indeed
Sidney was reasonably familiar with Platonic philosophy: references to Plato in *Astrophil and Stella* and in the

Apology make this plain enough.[16] But his notion of the artistic universal, probably borrowed from Fracastoro,[17] commits him to rather different aims than we notice in Ficino, where the progressive rationalization of visual experience leads the ambitious soul to a purely intellectual union with divine ideas or divinity itself. Sidney's less esoteric purpose is to propose moral concepts rendered in poetic form as necessary to the education of the will.

From one point of view, Sidney's universal is an abstraction from nature: it depicts typically proper or improper conduct and character by going beyond the natural particular: Lucrece, he points out, is better depicted as the visible embodiment of grief than as a historical individual (102. 30–33). Sharing the views of Barbaro, he credits the poet with offering "a familiar insight into anger" (108. 5), that is, neither a representation of this or that angry man nor an analytic discussion of the passion; not Cyrus as the historian would attempt to recover him, but an invented Cyrus, as Cyrus ought to be, in order to move the reader to emulation, "to bestow a Cyrus upon the world to make many Cyruses, if they will learn aright why and how that maker made him" (101. 11–13). Therefore, when Sidney brings up the issue of the poet's "*Idea* or fore-conceit," we perhaps ought to hesitate before concluding that he means a concept innocent of material imagery or representation, a Platonic abstraction initially "invented" as such. He says:

> . . . for any understanding knoweth the skill of the artificer standeth in that *Idea* or fore-conceit of the work, and not in the work itself. And that the poet hath that *Idea* is manifest,

by delivering *them* forth in such excellency as he hath imagined *them*. (101. 2–7)

The pronouns I have italicized refer not to *Idea* (which is italicized in the text) but to a list which immediately precedes the quotation: "so true a lover as Theagenes, so constant a friend as Pylades, so valiant a man as Orlando, so right a prince as Xenophon's Cyrus, so excellent a man every way as Virgil's Aeneas" (100. 36–39). Moveover, Sidney's use of "imagined" for what goes on in the poet's mind before he commits his thoughts to paper is a reasonable guarantee that the act of poetic conception includes material imagery. Nor is the reader invited, as Forrest Robinson maintains, to reverse the process in his own mind and rationalize the imagery of fiction by abandoning its sensory garment and returning it to the abstracted order of philosophy.[18] The poet's task is to conceive and commit to paper a union of idea and image, and it is this composite entity that should enter the reader's mind and stay fixed within it.

The *Apology* offers a supremely clear statement of this point:

Only let Aeneas be worn in the tablet of your memory, how he governeth himself in the ruin of his country; in the preserving his old father, and carrying away his religious ceremonies; in obeying the god's commandment to leave Dido, though not only all passionate kindness, but even human consideration of virtuous gratefulness, would have craved other of him; how in storms, how in sports, how in war, how in peace, how a fugitive, how victorious, how beseiged, how beseiging, how to strangers, how to allies, how to enemies, how to his own; lastly, how in his inward self, and how in his outward government; and I think, in a

> mind not prejudiced with a prejudicating humour, he will
> be found in excellency fruitful, yea, even as Horace saith,
> *melius Chrysippo et Crantore.* (119. 30—120. 5)

It is Aeneas, not an abstraction, who is to be worn in the
tablet of the memory, for the will is best moved by
images.[19] Sidney as much as admits that Platonic ideas
may also be moving when he cites Plato and Tully to the
effect that "who could see virtue would be wonderfully
ravished with love of her beauty" (119. 20—21), but he is
careful to add that the poet "sets her out to make her
more lovely in her holiday apparel" (120. 22—23).[20]
What the poet offers is a superior power of sustained
clarity and sharp affect:

> Now doth the peerless poet perform both: for whatsoever
> the philosopher saith should be done, he giveth a perfect
> picture of it in some one by whom he presupposeth it was
> done, so as he coupleth the general notion with the particu-
> lar example. A perfect picture I say, *for he yieldeth to the
> powers of the mind an image* of that whereof the philosopher
> bestoweth but a wordish description, which doth neither
> strike, pierce, nor possess the sight of the soul so much as
> that other doth. (107. 9—17; italics added)

I take Sidney's phrase "the sight of the soul" to refer to
the imagination, for once it resides in this faculty an
image is accessible to all the other powers, and especially
the feelings.[21] Particular emotions, as well as particular
categories of experience, are both portrayed in and
called forth by the established genres, each in its own
fashion. Sidney's account of the pastoral fails to mention
the kind of response it should provoke, but it does
exhibit misery, the blessedness of a humble existence,

"considerations of wrongdoing and patience" (116. 20–21), and so forth. Comedy implies a kind of emotional detachment, though perhaps ridicule and scorn are to be inferred (117. 12–13, 26–29). The elegaic is calculated to move pity, and the iambic "rubs the galled mind, in making shame the trumpet of villainy with bold and open crying out against naughtiness" (116. 34–36). The satiric provokes laughter, but tragedy stirs "the affects of admiration and commiseration," and Sidney here records an anecdote about the tyrant Alexander Pheraeus "from whose eyes a tragedy well made and represented, drew abundance of tears . . ." (118. 9–10). (Perhaps the example is ill-chosen, for Sidney concedes that Alexander was too hard-hearted to change his own habits.) The lyric, especially useful for praise, moves even in its simplest form, and songs are noted in martial societies as "the chiefest kindlers of brave courage" (118. 33). More generally the lyric "is that kind most capable and most fit to awake the thoughts from the sleep of idleness, to embrace honourable enterprises" (119. 9–11), but above all the images of heroic character "most inflameth the mind with desire to be worthy, and informs with counsel how to be worthy" (119. 29–30).

With nearly total consistency Sidney ascribes an emotional effect to each kind and even hints that the genres may be ranked by the relative value of the emotional responses they are designed to prompt in the audience. As Sidney describes these responses they must be seen as common human feelings. The audience proposed for literature is every bit as universal as the images that confront it. Indeed Sidney's concept of such an audience is certainly one of the reasons he dwells so persistently on moving as the task of literature. The poet to some

extent seeks a reproduction in the reader's sensibility of
states of feeling portrayed or expressed in art, but more
important is the proposed assault on the will, the active
instrument of choice which prompts and schools the
feelings, directing them either to embrace or avoid the
conditions found in the poem. There is no attempt
totally to isolate a single faculty of the mind, for the kind
of willed assent that literature calls for is a response of
the whole mind. Nevertheless, the feelings must have a
kind of priority:

> And that moving is of a higher degree than teaching, it
> may by this appear, that it is well nigh the cause and effect
> of teaching. For who will be taught, if he be not moved with
> desire to be taught? and what so much good doth that
> teaching bring forth (I speak still of moral doctrine) as that
> it moveth one to do that which it doth teach? For, as
> Aristotle saith, it is not *gnosis* but *praxis* must be the fruit.
> And how *praxis* cannot be, without being moved to prac-
> tise, it is no hard matter to consider. (112. 30–38)

As Sidney employs the term here, "moving" draws
into its significance all the several stages of affective
response which he tries to bring to our notice, and it is
worth recalling once more that these are possible even if
the doctrine a poet urges on his reader is false. Poetry
can misdirect the will, and in that respect the poet's
rationality is essential. But among the faculties both poet
and reader must employ, the reason is almost for Sidney
a given. His notorious confidence in our "erected wit"
leads him to a statement about natural reason which
suggests that man's problem is not the state of his moral
knowledge, but his desire to act upon it: "But to be

moved to do that which we know, or to be moved with desire to know, *hoc opus, hic labor est*" (113. 15—17). This is a weak point in Sidney's argument, no matter how commonplace the doctrine,[22] for it is odd that on the one hand he can propose that poetry is a superior form of learning, leading to a knowledge we do not yet possess, and on the other hand support his contempt for philosophers by saying that "in Nature we know it is well to do well, and what is well and what is evil" (113. 12—13). This is a contradiction Sidney lets stand in his eagerness to focus attention on the peculiar gifts of poetry.

These gifts amount to the poet's ability to bring doctrine to life, to quicken precept by the palpability of example, to "bestow that in colours upon you which is fittest for the eye to see: as the constant though lamenting look of Lucretia, when she punished in herself another's fault; wherein he painteth not Lucretia whom he never saw, but painteth the outward beauty of such a virtue" (102. 29—33). Released from the necessity merely to copy nature, the poet is bound by no law but wit. "Wit" is a term of varying significance,[23] but in this context it emphasizes the poet's imagination, or, it would be well to note, an inventive freedom to "range, only reined with learned discretion, into the divine consideration of what may be and should be" (102. 36—37). The constraint of such logic and the added constraint of artistic propriety urge the poet towards what is tuned to the faculties of the audience. On the level of style, "those words which are fittest for memory are likewise most convenient for knowledge" (122. 10—11), but much more important is "this imagining of matters . . . so fit for the imagination" (109. 19—20). This phrase, which occurs as Sidney prepares to answer the objection that history offers a better grasp of truth than poetry, has a double significance: first, it seems to evoke the capacity of the imagination to envisage the non-existent ("forms such as never were in Nature" [100. 24–25]); second, it may imply nearly the reverse, images suited to our imagination precisely because they do not really lead it astray, because they combine the sufficiently fictional with the fundamentally and universally truthful. Sidney, I think, settles on the second meaning, even as he leads us to recognize the poet's capacity to employ imagination irresponsibly. Fitness, moreover, is a technical as well as a moral concept.

The reader's imagination in Sidney's lexicon is, as I have indicated earlier, both a faculty able to accept representations and a capacity for turning the verbal into the visual. It may also be stretched to suggest the value or status of the image. At one point he remarks, "Truly, for myself, me seems I see before my eyes the lost child's disdainful prodigality, turned to envy a swine's dinner" (109. 7–9), which is another way of saying that inner sight, feeding on the memory of what is read, accepts the vividness or actuality of the recollected image. This power of authenticity carries with it the obligation of restraint, and if Sidney's language often seems to liberate the poet from nature and the reader from systematic logical thought, the general drift of his argument is to limit the poet's discretion bit by bit, to plead for what Harry Berger calls "controlled fantasy and artifice."[24] But that control is not aimed at the reader's capacity for cool, judicious reason, or at least not primarily. Sidney's didacticism is conventional only up to a point, for there is substantial originality in the weight and attention he gives to the need to manage the affective nature of the literary audience. His very pointed retreat from philosophy, no matter how overstated it may appear, is not just a talking point: it is quite coordinate with a proposal to dignify the sensory vividness of art as the means to school the feelings.

V

Verisimilar Things: Tasso's Discourses on the Heroic Poem *(1594)*

Torquato Tasso and Sidney were near contemporaries and in a number of ways alike. Both valued and practiced the epic genre; as critics both profited from nearly two centuries of Humanist doctrine and pondered very carefully the ways in which poetry might be supposed to influence the reader. Both are basically didactic critics, and like Sidney Tasso can be understood to belong to the mode of didacticism we have been examining. But if Tasso could generally argue that the end of poetry was to please, move, and instruct an audience, he grounded his argument on a very different view of what an audience would find credible and persuasive, and it is at this point of departure that our interest in his theory begins.

The differences between Tasso and Sidney can be followed a bit further. For most of the *Apology* Sidney ignores the problem of verisimilitude and whether or not an audience requires it. Freed from history as Sidney chose to define it, the poet could tune his invention to what would best school the reader's mind and will; only when he comes to discuss the quality of contemporary English literature does Sidney turn to "natural rules" and elementary credibility as standards of artistic value.[1] Tasso, on the other hand, found himself committed to a positive family relationship between poetry (especially heroic poetry) and history, and this commitment threads its way through his more mature critical writings, inevitably qualifying the way he understands the connections between poetic form and audience reception. The line of critical thought represented by Fracastoro, Barbaro, and Sidney generally stressed the fictional or "made up" and this more often than not implied a departure from factual or historical truth in order to make moral truth both evident and appealing.

Tasso proposes instead that fiction must be intimately tied to history, indeed grounded firmly in it. He contemplates an audience more sensitive to fact and less willing to respond ubiquitously to the improbable or incredible. Though perhaps more literal-minded than Sidney's "willing hearer," Tasso's audience is also more sophisticated, demanding that the fabulous be referred to carefully rationalized causes. For Tasso and for the kind of reader he imagines, truth is bound into history, not divorced from it, and this view makes his criticism transitional, marking the beginning of the end of a kind of theory that can postulate a largely universal, undifferentiated audience. It is in the light that his criticism merits our attention.

Tasso's concern for history appears in the very early *Discorsi del Arte Poetica* (composed in the 1560s and published in 1587). Here he argues that historical character and event must in some fashion be the source of the heroic poem, the backbone of its fable, and the means to its credibility and contact with truth. Tasso concedes that the poet may find his argument either in his own invention or in history, but it is much better, he thinks, that it be drawn from history. This is so because the epic poet must always seek verisimilitude, and the illustrious actions that are appropriate to such poems only gain their status in the memory with the aid of history.[2] The immediate context of these observations is Tasso's objection to the fanciful indifference of Ariosto to historical and natural fact, but there is also a deeper reason for his preference and this emerges in the paragraph immediately following the one I have just paraphrased: he is primarily concerned with what an audience will believe, and thus he is willing to place restrictions upon the epic or tragic poet which the comic poet need not observe.

> For this reason, since the poet ought to beguile his readers with the semblance of truth, and not only persuade them that the things which he treats are true, but submit them in such a way to their senses that they believe not just that they are reading but that they are present and seeing and hearing, it is necessary to effect in their souls this opinion of truth, which easily happens through the authority of history: I speak of those poets who imitate illustrious actions, the tragic and the epic; for the comic poet, who is the imitator of ignoble and popular actions is always allowed to invent his argument according to his wish.[3]

The later *Discorsi del Poema Eroico*, with which this chapter will be primarily concerned, represents a considerable sophistication of such pronouncements as this, but Tasso never abandoned the conviction he exhibits here—that the poet's obligation is to be believable. The comic poet is allowed to make up his stories because private events can always be made to seem verisimilar, but Tasso's interest in what he obviously considers an inferior form of literature is not very great. The more elevated forms require a genuine or at least a plausible origin in reality if they are to do their job; for this reason the palpable impossibilities of Ariosto are inappropriate in modern epic. Thus an important element in Tasso's thought is sensitive to the pressures exerted by the influence of Aristotle's mimetic doctrine. One of the results, even in the theory of those such as Castelvetro, who disagreed pointedly with Aristotle, was an effort to locate those parts of a poem which would indeed attract and move an audience. Castelvetro wrote that the end of poetry "has been found solely to delight and recreate; and I say to delight and recreate the minds of the vulgar multitude and common people."[4] Such an audience is insensitive to subtle argument, so poetry "ought to have as its subject matter those things which can be understood by the common people and which, when understood, make them happy."[5] Poetry must also be verisimilar and resemble history, but this is not the source of delight. The simple reproduction of history would omit those qualities of the marvelous and partially unfamiliar by which an audience is moved. Castelvetro postulates audiences without imagination or depth and able to believe only what is most immediately in front of them: here, to take one example, is the basis for his

justification for the unity of time.[6] Such audiences re-
lentlessly measure the fortunes of literary characters
against their own experience. Spectators in search of
pacification and entertainment, they do not require instruction and reform.[7]

Castelvetro's extreme, and for his age eccentric, concentration on poetry as a vulgar art is, of course, quite
different from Tasso's position, but the attachment of
each to some form of verisimilitude forces them to
consider similar problems which they solve in very
different ways. Tasso's is the more complicated because
he is unwilling to abandon certain other theoretical
imperatives he has had to adjust to the claims of Aristo-
telianism. Having committed himself to a Neoplatonic
system of metaphysics and concerned in the traditional
way that poetry offer ethically responsible doctrine to its
readers, he seeks to reconcile these obligations to the
claims of verisimilitude. And to complicate matters
further he is also aware, like Castelvetro, of a contemporary audience whose expectations might be very different from those of the ancient Greeks or Romans.

The various threads of Tasso's thinking come together
most maturely in the treatise published in 1494, a year
before his death, *Discorsi del Poema Eroico (Discourses on
the Heroic Poem)*, a fairly lengthy treatise divided into six
books which moves from the most general questions
about the nature and purposes of poetry to more specific
matters of plot, character, and style. His first words
express his awareness of the needs of an audience, but
in contrast to earlier Humanist references to an undifferentiated readership, Tasso seems to appeal directly to
an aristocratic sensibility:

Heroic poems, and discussions of the art and mode of composing them, should naturally interest no one more than those who enjoy reading about deeds like their own and their ancestors' because in such poems they may see an image, as it were, of the very glory that gets them considered superior to others. Recognizing the virtues of their fathers and forefathers as made, if not more beautiful, at least more various and illustrious by poetry, they try to raise their own minds to its example; and their intellect itself becomes a painter who, following its pattern, paints in their souls forms of courage, temperance, prudence, justice, faith, piety, religion, and every other virtue that may be acquired by long practice or infused by divine grace.[8]

The cultivation of an elite or the suggestion that the heroic poem deals only in patterns of virtue are less important than Tasso's sense of the way the mind should use poetry: "their intellect itself becomes a painter." Through the medium of the poem, the reader is the artist of his own virtue. Tasso begins, in other words, with an understanding of the end of poetry very much like Sidney's. And like Sidney he seems to settle for a human, rather than a divine, poetry. The painter may paint gods, but really he "paints nothing but a human or animal form, since he cannot imitate divinity. . . . The difference between the imitator of divine and human things is thus as great as that between ideas proper and what we call images and likenesses" (p. 9). It is not that the divine and conceptual are to be ignored; rather they must be presented in material and active form, and behind this assertion there lies both the kind of epistemology familiar in Dante—divine truth may

only be represented in images tailored to the limitations
of the human intellect—and the authority of Aristotle: "I
would therefore conclude that poetry is nothing but an
imitation of human actions, which are properly imitable,
and that all others are imitated not in themselves but by
accident, and not as principal but as accessory" (p. 10).
And a few pages later there is a still further narrowing of
the ground—in conventional fashion not any human
actions are to be imitated but those that suit moral
instruction; poetry is designed "to teach us how to live"
and "will deal with moral habit and with thought, which
the Greeks called 'διάνοια' " (p. 19).

Once he begins to consider pleasure, however, Tasso
becomes less exact. Though he is certain that the aim of
poetry is moral betterment, he is undecided how central
pleasure is. He admits its presence and even appears to
agree with Isocrates that Homer and the tragic poets
aimed their language "entirely to delight." "It may be,"
he adds, "that pleasure directed to usefulness is the end
of poetry" (p. 10), and a few sentences later he says,
"We should at least grant that the end of poetry is not
just any enjoyment but only that which is coupled with
virtue, since it is entirely unworthy of a good poet to
give the pleasure of reading about base and dishonest
deeds, but proper to give the pleasure of learning
together with virtue" (p. 11). Tasso is, I think, facing
what is for him a genuine problem: in his Aristotelian
mood he inherits the belief that happiness is an end in
itself and states that, because the useful has an end
beyond itself, "it is a less noble purpose than pleasure
and has less resemblance to the final purpose" (p. 11).
This is not, however, a position that he can hold

securely, and after attempting to deal with Fracastoro's notion that the poet is primarily concerned with the idea of the beautiful (p. 13), he decides that poetry gives profit through delight, "so that the delight may get us to read more willingly" (p. 14). Tasso has brought himself, and us, back to the traditional recognition that poetry will not have its way unless it is in some fashion attractive and compelling.

This topic is worth our attention because it is a stage in Tasso's progress towards what for him had been a perennial question: how can the heroic poem be mimetically accurate and at the same time moving? In the early *Discorsi del Arte Poetica* he had rejected the notion that the verisimilar and the marvelous should be separate and distinct elements in the same poem, insisting instead that he "held the epic poet to a perpetual obligation to observe the verisimilar" but did not "therefore excuse him from the other part, which is the marvelous; thus I judge that the same action can be both marvelous and verisimilar."[9] It turns out, of course, that he is talking about incidents that derive from angelic or divine intervention, such as many of those in his own poem. The later treatise, in offering a substantially greater attention to affect, gives a great deal more weight to the marvelous as a source of the epic poem's appeal. Tasso is more attentive in the *Discourses on The Heroic Poem* to genre and to the different impacts each may have than he was in the earlier essay and than, say, Sidney, who recognized the peculiarities of each genre and then went on to argue that they all had a common end achieved by different means. Tasso separates the major kinds of poem according to their ends:

Now the end of each ought to be peculiar to it: as the art of
making bridles has one aim and that of making halberds has
another, although both are subordinated to the art of war
and directed to the goal it sets, in the same way tragedy
should have one end, comedy another, the epic poem
another still—or another effect since the form of each thing
is distinguished by its proper effect. Now the effect of
tragedy is to purge the soul by terror and compassion,[10]
and that of comedy is to move laughter at base things . . .
The epic poem ought therefore to afford its own delight with
its own effect—which is perhaps to move wonder, an effect
that seems far from peculiar to it, since tragedy too moves
wonder. . . . (P. 15)

So, Tasso continues, does comedy. How then is the epic
poem to be distinguished from other kinds? First, in the
means it chooses. "We gladly read in epic about many
wonders that might be unsuitable on stage, both because
they are proper to epic and because the reader allows
many liberties which the spectator forbids" (p. 16). The
result of this incomplete argument is to focus attention
on the manner and means of the reader's response. If
the same terms may be applied to several kinds of affect
produced by several kinds of poem, nevertheless a
system of priorities will help avoid collapsing all genres
back into a single category. "Moreover," Tasso continues, "other kinds of poem move wonder in order to
move laughter or compassion or some other emotion.
But the epic in fact moves it more powerfully and more
often" (p. 17). He then concludes this stage of the
argument with a definition of epic: "We shall then say
that the epic poem is an imitation of a noble action, great
and perfect, narrated in the loftiest verse, with the
purpose of moving the mind to wonder and thus being

useful" (p. 17). Wonder is another term for delight, or better, its highest form, and Tasso is here conflating delight and utility, as he is to do with some consistency throughout the *Discourses*. In Book III, while discussing *dianoia* or "discourse," he notes that it should, as Aristotle says, deal with "universal matters—not all of them, however, but just those that pertain to action and are to be chosen or rejected" (p. 91). We must also remember that he locates poetry in the broad category of moral philosophy.

Nevertheless, the continuing weight of his attention is given to wonder or delight, not to questions of the moral betterment of the audience, which is generally assumed.[11] Thus Book III, which deals with the subject matter of the epic poem—Tasso takes up such topics as piety or revenge, for example—constantly turns into a treatment of means. These are in turn handled according to a persistent notion of what the sensibility of the audience requires. In discussing methods of proof, one of which is the maxim, he remarks of one example that "it proves or confutes with marvelous effect on the feelings" (p. 92). And in Virgil's Turnus "we see the image of the moral habit of a young man"; indeed "the moral habits of men old and young, and of women too, amid the dangers of war are virtually made into a picture . . ." (p. 100). One might almost conclude that Tasso is, under another guise, discussing *enargeia*,[12] and the conclusion seems accurate enough when we read of *dianoia* that its "parts" are "to demonstrate, to solve, to arouse emotions such as compassion, wrath, or fear, to magnify and diminish, or to make known the greatness or smallness of things" (p. 90).

Before proceeding any further with Tasso's theories

about delight, it is necessary to return to verisimilitude, which occupies an almost equally central position in his thought about literature and the way it is informed by the nature of the audience. In the *Discorsi del Arte Poetica* this was the subject of the first discourse; in the later essay the attention to the audience marks a substantial difference in emphasis. Verisimilitude occupies most of his attention in Book II, and he takes it as seriously, especially in this final verson of his critical thought, as any of the Italians who based their systems on Aristotle's *Poetics*.

Tasso begins by repeating the common analogy between material or sensible things and the immaterial: " . . . in intellectual things too something can be found resembling matter, that may, by analogy, or proportion as we may wish to put it, be called by the same name." The name is "matter" or "material." "We not only, therefore, speak of the matter of a speech, a syllogism, or a verse, but also call material a capacity of our intellect apt to receive all forms" (p. 21). The matter of poetry is immense and various, and therefore the task of the poet, who must be "prudent," is threefold: to choose matter that is fitted to receive form; to give it form; and then to deck it out with ornament. Unlike the orator, who is allowed in certain cases to tailor his remarks to the occasion and even distort the truth, the poet has an obligation at least to appear accurate, especially in suiting his treatment to the moral nature of his material.

> Hence, let us assume that with equal skill and eloquence one person wishes to move compassion for Oedipus, who unwittingly killed his father, and another for Medea, who, consciously wicked, destroyed her children. The fable woven from the misfortunes of Oedipus will turn out much

more pitiful than that made of Medea's bestial resolution. That will inflame us with pity, this hardly warms us. (P. 25)

This remark offers a clue to a distinction Tasso makes elsewhere between those elements in a poem which ought to be constant and those that can be varied according to time and custom. Eloquence is variable and a matter of the poet's discretion, but not to the point where it would violate our basic moral sense. Insofar as we would pity Oedipus and be repelled by Medea, our feelings are in harmony with universal truth, and the connection Tasso is seeking between truth and the response of the audience can be established. There is an inference that, however different a modern world might be from the antique, this moral and emotional equation between image and response would remain stable and fundamental.

But Tasso is also conscious of the nature of historical memory, which imposes certain limitations upon the poet. He may invent his material or draw it from history. In the times before there was history, poets depended upon report, eyewitness accounts, or common opinion. But after Homer poets have tended to take their material from history; indeed Tasso thinks it almost impossible to invent things because "by now all memorable actions have been written of, so that any not written of do not seem worth remembering" (p. 25). Tasso is, of course, talking about the epic or heroic poet: the kind of action and event that is proper to his poem is likely to have been recorded historically.

Great and eventful actions cannot be unknown; where they are not recorded, from this fact alone men argue their falsity. And when they think them false they do not easily accept writings, which otherwise would move them now to anger, now to pity, now to fear, now would sadden them, now fill them with empty lightness, now hold them in suspense, now in rapture. In short, men do not await the end of the story with the same expectation as when they deem it true entirely or in part. For when we do not credit things we can have little feeling for or take little pleasure in what we read or hear. But the poet, who is to deceive the reader with the semblance of truth, commonly delights him with the variety of his lies. . . .[13] None the less the poet seeks to persuade us that what he treats deserves belief and credit; he makes an effort to gain such belief and credit through the authority of history and renowned names and to win good will by praising virtue and valorous men, since, as Plato says, it is dangerous to be hated. (I mean those who imitate illustrious deeds, the tragic and the epic poet.) And Aristotle's authority confirms this: if poets are imitators, it is fitting that they imitate truth, since the false does not exist, and what does not exist cannot be imitated. Those who write what is wholly false, then, not being imitators, are not poets, and their com- positions are not poems but rather fictions; hence they either do not deserve, or deserve far less, the name of poet. (Pp. 26–27)

This extraordinary statement deserves some scrutiny. First of all it rests on a view of the human mind which has it demanding circumstantial truth or its appearance as the price of emotional assent; second, it seems to accept the persuasive lie (fiction must not appear to be fiction and must be mixed with fact); third, it indulges in rather obviously fallacious reasoning (poets must be imitators; they must imitate truth, because the false does not exist; therefore those who write what is false, are not poets); and fourth, it denies fiction to poetry. One might well ask how the false can be written about, if it does not exist: Tasso seems to be conceding that there is a realm of phantastic invention but that, since it deals with neither circumstantial nor conceptual truth, it is not true poetry.[14] He is aiming at two important targets. In the first place he wants to deny status to poetry that employs the obviously monstrous and unnatural (hippogriffs and chimeras and the like); and in the second place he seeks to base poetry firmly on the mental faculties he associates with dialectic and rhetoric: "I say, therefore, that poetry surely belongs under dialectic along with rhetoric, which, as Aristotle says, is the other child of the dialectical faculty, its function being to consider not the false but the probable" (p. 29).

It is in this context that he makes his famous attack on Mazzoni for including poetry in the category of phantastic imitation.[15] Mazzoni had argued at some length that poets like Dante could indeed be called imitators because the concepts of the mind are imitable, just as external natural or historical fact is. The images or idols of the phantastic imitator can be referred back to truth allegorically. Mazzoni has little to say about the effects of poetry, but he does qualify the apparent license he gives to the poet as a fabricator of phantastic images. The older form of sophistic, under which he classifies poetry, is not suspect:

> The other species of sophistic is that which Philostratus called the old sophistic and which, though it does offer feigned things to the intellect, does not mislead the will, but wholly and in every way tries to make it conform to what is just. . . . Now I say that phantastic poetry regulated by proper rules is part of the old sophistic, since it also submits feigned things to our intellect to control the

appetite and many times contains the truth of many noble
concepts under the surface of the fiction.[16]

Superficially Mazzoni's argument seems both more lucid
and more plausible than Tasso's, and it appears to
accommodate a much greater range of poetic practice.
However, it depends upon a number of assertions that
remain just that: poets aren't really lying; they do not
mislead the will; fiction appeals to our intellect and
moderates appetite; one need only read it allegorically.
But even Mazzoni has to qualify some of this. He has
stated flatly that the poet always deals with the credible,
and this forces him to concede that it is sometimes
necessary "to use individual and sensible means to
represent the things about which he writes, whatever
they may be." He then adds, "And when he treats
things pertinent to contemplative doctrine, he ought to
make every effort to represent them with idols and
sensible simulacra. . . ."[17] Mazzoni is deeply committed
to conventions of rationalizing certain freedoms in poetic
method, assuming the fundamental necessity of the
appeal to the reader's sensible imagination, and pre-
scribing a moral and doctrinal probity. And with all this
he must admit that it is possible to compose poetry that
belongs to the "new" sophistic, "and is such that it
disorders the appetite with immoderate pleasure and
makes it in every way rebellious to reason and also
causes damage and harm to virtuous living."[18] Where-
ever the Renaissance theorist turns he is answerable
both to the moral imperatives of his time and to the
apparently ineradicable connection between the imagery
of art and man's sensible, passionate nature.

Tasso registers vigorous objections to Mazzoni's

classification of poetry as sophistic and to the indeterminate doctrinal reference of his imagery:

> On grounds of verisimilitude, then, none of these elements [centaurs, harpies, and cyclopes] alone constitutes the adequate subject of poetry, as Mazzoni thinks. Nor does he prove it by his argument that poetry is the maker of idols, ergo poetry is sophistry; not only because it is wrong to have two affirmative propositions in a second-figure syllogism, but also because the term *idols* has various meanings and, depending on how it is defined, the creation of idols may belong either to the poet or to the sophist. (P. 31)

The difference is not just that of definition, but also of origin and reference: "But when we affirm that the poet is a maker of idols we do not mean only idols of non existent things, since the poet imitates existing things and indeed represents them principally" (p. 31). Tasso's persistent assertions tie the poet to the existing and true, and because he firmly believes in a teleological connection between the immaterial and material, he sees a necessary connection between what the poet chooses to imitate and his own definition of poetry as a form of dialectic. Thus his reaction to Mazzoni's classification of poetry as a form of sophistic is founded in his sense of the poet's relationship to truth and its manifestations in the external world, not in the nature of the imagery itself. He is perfectly ready to concede the validity of "the winged lion, the eagle, ox, and angel, which are images of the evangelists" (p. 32), but not of "Tritons, Sphinxes, and Centaurs" (p. 31). The first are the products of true spiritual vision seated in "the indivisible mind" (p. 31);[19] the second are apparently products of

the imagination of the sensitive soul and hence phantastic images, deceptive appearances, in the derogatory
sense of the term supplied by Plato. In other words, if it
is Christian truth the poet seeks to embody in his
images, those images are verisimilar, not because they
imitate the facts of history or nature but because they
refer to what is intellectually or spiritually valid. If, to the
contrary, the poet invents incredible beings and unnatural occurrences, these refer neither to intellectual
truth nor to nature or history and they are therefore to be
denied the label of poetry. This distinction admits of one
important qualification: poets must cater to the sense of
truth in their own times. Depictions of the gentile gods
are verisimilar because when they were composed they
were believed to be true. A modern poet cannot make
this claim (pp. 38–39). At one blow the method of a
great deal of allegorical symbolism is discarded: the
relationship between an image and the concept it embodies or refers to must be one of similitude, and a
rather self-evident similitude at that, except where
Christian symbolism is concerned. There is no possibility of Tasso's objecting to the methods of Scripture,
but he feels quite free to object to equivalent symbolic
method if its referent is "pagan," and he will not
concede that classical mythology, for example, can be
used with self-conscious and open symbolic intent by a
Christian poet.

But we are still left holding Tasso's allegiance to
history as the matter of epic poetry, and we may well
wonder how that squares with the following passage:

> But what shall we say exists, the intelligible or the visible?
> Surely the intelligible, in the opinion of Plato too, who put

visible things in the genus of non-being and only the intelligible in the genus of being. (P. 32)

Thus even though Tasso tentatively suggests an intellectual as well as a sensitive phantasy to buttress his argument, he is still faced with problems that this line of reasoning will not resolve. So he returns to questions of the nature of the heroic poem itself. This involves shifting the ground for discussing what is true and false in poetry from ontological to formal questions. Bound to value poems drawn fundamentally from historical events, he limits invention and novelty to the mode of treatment.

> The poet, then, in some parts is friendly to truth, which he illuminates and embellishes with new colours and may be said to transform from old to antique to new. The poem is new when the weaving of the complication is new, its resolution new, and all the episodes in between new, even if the material is thoroughly known and has been treated before by others. For the novelty of the poem occurs in the form rather than in the material. (P. 34)

Such a program, especially if the poet avoids "the actions of the pagans," will satisfy the need for the verisimilar and credible, which Tasso does not wish to be derived from "the verse and other ornaments" (pp. 34–35).

Tasso's interest in such a division of labor is the consequence of his belief that the epic poem must be at once credible and marvelous. The epic poet has to convince his readers that the incidents in his poem have a fundamental connection with truth; at the same time he has to dazzle them, for wonder, the form of delight appropriate to the epic, is necessary if the poem is to be moving. Yet these qualities are difficult to yoke into the same harness, and Tasso does not wish to achieve either through the somewhat dangerous medium of ornament.

> But now let us pursue our argument as to how the verisimilar may be combined with the marvellous, without the grace and charm of verse to persuade the ear like so many enticements. The verisimilar and the marvellous are very different in nature . . . different almost to the point of being antithetical. . . . (P. 37)

He does not wish to separate the two, leaving one element in the poem to account for the verisimilar and another for the marvelous, and he is unwilling to agree that some part of a poem can depart from the verisimilar. Poetry, he repeats, is imitation, and no imitation can be achieved without making a resemblance. Imitation is not a matter of ornamental discretion; it is "proper and intrinsic."

The marvelous derives from actions that exceed human power, and such actions can be attributed "to God, to his angels, to demons, or to those granted power by God or by demons, for example, saints, wizards, and fairies. Such actions, if considered in themselves, will seem marvellous; nay, they are commonly called miracles. But if regarded in terms of their agent's efficacy and power, they will seem verisimilar" (p. 38). Restricted to Christian example, such departures from the usual workings of nature will seem familiar:

> For men, having drunk in this notion along with their milk from the time they were in swaddling clothes, and

having been confirmed in it by the teachers of our holy
faith (that is, God and his ministers, and by his permission
demons and magicians, can do marvellous things beyond
the force of nature), and reading and hearing of new examples daily, will not think unlikely what they believe not
only is possible but has often occurred and can occur often
again. (P. 38)

There is no avoiding the parochialism of Tasso's rather
strained reasoning, even though we may concede a
readiness to believe in miracle and magic more suited to
his age than to our own. What he is saying is that events
that are astounding can be construed as believable,
when his argument would be better served by a demonstration, if that were possible, that more common varieties of verisimilitude could compel wonder as well as
belief. Instead, his point is to urge the avoidance of
classical mythology in those elements of plot where the
supernatural enters. And this is less bizarre than his
language might indicate, if we concede his point that the
aim of heroic poetry is to "kindle the souls" of Christian
knights on the grounds that "the precedent of people
like oneself [is] far more moving than that of different
people . . ." (p. 39).

However clumsily, Tasso is aware of the importance of
a contemporary culture for the reception of the contemporary poet, but he concedes that "modern stories"
may "remove the freedom to invent and imitate, which
is essential to poets, particularly epic poets" (p. 40).
Some compromise between the remote and the familiar
is necessary, and Tasso settles for "things neither too
new nor too old" as the material for the successful epic
poem (p. 41). But the means he finds to resolve the

problem are less important for this study than his awareness of a particular and contemporary audience conditioned by its own peculiar experience and by a set of
religious and intellectual commitments quite different
from those of the early audiences of Homer and Virgil.
His admission of love into the heroic poem is important
evidence of his sensitivity to his own times—love not
only "as a passion and movement of the sensitive
appetite, but a highly noble habit of the will, as St.
Thomas held . . ." (p. 47).

Tasso is confronting a problem similar to that behind
the contradiction in Sidney's acknowledgment of the
poet's inventive freedom on the one hand and his scorn
of the products of that freedom in the drama written by
his British contemporaries on the other. Although Tasso
never concedes to the poet the measure of imaginative
license Sidney would allow for the sake of the ideal, he
does wish to locate what is most fundamental in the
poem in a form of ideal truth. This belief is stated as
plainly as anywhere else in the very late but undated
*Giudizio sovra La Sua Gerusalemme da Lui Medesimo Rifor-
mata*, in which he cites Plato's *Laws* to the effect that
imitation ought to be of the most beautiful things and
adds that the verisimilar image in poetry ought to be like
the exemplar, not an image of a particular man or prince
but of "the idea of man or of the good prince."[20] Tasso
acknowledges a truth independent of different eras and
cultures which demands universal recognition, but now
in the *Discorsi* we find him suggesting as well that
Christian indoctrination and cultural experience dispose
the mind to accept or reject certain poetic events. Thus
another kind of fidelity is also required—a fidelity to
historical and circumstantial authenticity—and this can-

not be divorced either from true doctrine or from what a contemporary audience can be brought to believe. The real end of poetry as delight is qualified to admit only the sort that is useful, but although the source of delight may be found in the basically truthful yet marvelous action the poet must imitate, the reader, Tasso says, is moved in the long run by the mode of treatment, by style understood in its broadest sense. Style is at the bottom of Tasso's hierarchy of poetic values;[21] yet his attention to it is prolonged. He does not quite match Fracastoro's conviction that ornament is what distinguishes poetic from other forms of discourse, but he comes close when he says, "Rather, the formal and final causes usually go together. . . . The end, therefore, is the form given by the skill of the poet, who, by adding, diminishing, and varying, disposes the matter and gives another aspect to the action and things he deals with" (p. 18).

Tasso returns to this question in the interesting remarks that open his final chapter, Book VI, dealing with levels of style. He seeks a Neoplatonic continuity between form and matter, and yet he is aware of difficulties, "For if we take the forms as separate entities, what the philosophers have called ideas, we may easily decide that they do not exist or that they are of no use to our human devices and mortal doings" (p. 171). He does not wish, in other words, to treat questions of manner and style as if they were abstract ideas, perhaps because he has indicated repeatedly that these are to some extent variable and subject to the choice of the poet. Indeed in Book III he confronts the notion of the absolute variability and neutral nature of words, that "they are man-made, so that they may signify this or that concept at man's pleasure" (p. 73), but at the same time the principles by which both nature and art function are constant (p. 74). He is unwilling, therefore, to accept an absolute relativism, but words, "ways of handling weapons," "sacrificial practises," and the like, do indeed take their quality from the times (p. 75). However, as Tasso pursues his list we discover that unity of fable and habits "that form our ethos" are constants (p. 75). Again in Book VI he appears to be eager to establish a "natural," that is constant, unity of form and matter for the epic, without separating them in "imagination" (p. 171), which would lead to falsehood or uselessness. Admitting that the task is difficult, he goes on to disagree with Fracastoro that all poetry aims at the idea of the beautiful. Rather the epic poem is especially marked by its capacity to move wonder, or in other terms to convey magnificence and solemnity (pp. 172–173).

In trying to sort out what is constant and what is variable, or to mediate between what is innately true and what is subject to the changes of custom, or to distinguish between what will always move men and what will only move them in their own time, Tasso, for all his hesitations and inconsistencies, is asking genuine questions. As a Neoplatonist he wants to discover in genre the "natural" mimetic relationship between the idea and the object; as a practical critic he must concern himself with matters that allow discretion to talent; and as both a follower of the followers of Aristotle and a rhetorician he must somehow adjust rules that seem necessary to formal excellence and the variables of organization and language. That Tasso has a difficult time with these concurrent roles may well be the result of his uniquely painful circumstances, but for us the difficulties are interesting because they emphasize the questions arising from the collision of various critical traditions, and they reveal above all what can happen in a body of theory which seeks to inform those traditions with a concept of the audience such as Tasso's.

This sense of the audience is complex, but we should recognize that it is in some ways orthodox. Tasso defines poetry as an imitation of human action fashioned so as to "teach us how to live" (p. 10). Like Sidney, he believes that this kind of moral instruction is best accomplished through the direct presentation of images of virtuous behavior, rather than through precept or demonstration (p. 32). It is at just this point that Tasso begins to deviate from some of the positions held by other critics we have examined. Unwilling, as we have seen, to accept Mazzoni's definition of poetry as a form of sophistry, he argues that the poetic image must be understood in a very different sense: "Wherefore, however much the poet is a maker of idols, that does not have to mean in the same sense as the sophist is called a maker of idols. Rather we should say that he is a maker of images in the fashion of a speaking painter, and in that is like the divine theologian who forms images and commands them to be" (p. 31). The poetic image appeals to the indivisible part of our mind, "which is intellect pure and simple" (p. 32). On this basis the poet (and presumably his reader) is in possession of an "intellectual imagination which cannot be differentiated from the icastic" (p. 33).[22] Tasso is leading us toward a concept of an audience that is on the one hand specialized and elite and on the other hand committed to a kind of fiction originating in history.

Yet, as we have also seen, the affective elements in the epic poem, indeed in any kind of poem, are not derived from history or the verisimilar. Instead, they are to be found in the ornament supplied by the skill of the poet. In the case of the epic or heroic poem, delight is wonder, and wonder is caused by the marvelous. At the same time, the cultivation of this kind of affective response cannot fly in the face of a kind of credibility:

> That is why I would put Charlemagne or Arthur as epic persons far ahead of Theseus or Jason. Finally, since the poet's great concern should be with improving men, he will kindle the souls of our knights much more with the example of the faithful than with that of infidels, the precedent of people like oneself being far more moving than that of different people and one's countrymen's more moving than strangers'. (P. 39)

This apparently describes the "icastic imagination" of the audience Tasso has in mind, though we should note that in subsequent pages he points out that examples drawn from places and events that are contemporary and close to home leave little room for invention and ornament precisely because they are too familiar. In any case, the tendencies Tasso represents anticipate certain Neoclassical esthetic positions, especially the conviction that audiences will be best pleased by imitations of things neither too remote nor too close to hand and the belief in a kind of wonder drawn from miracles or prodigies compatible with the logic of Christian belief.

Above all Tasso's concerns show the influence of the *Poetics* on didactic theory. It would be quite incorrect to suggest that earlier Italian critics, such as Fracastoro, were more interested in poetic ornament than in truth. Rather they tended to think that truth could appear convincingly in rather improbable fictional form. But later sixteenth-century readings of Aristotle began to establish a kind of rationalistic orthodoxy, one that emphasized rules, regularity, credibility, and probability; or, if these qualities had not exactly been hardened into dogma, the wind was blowing in that direction, and Tasso was sensitive to it. On the authority of Aristotle he has begun to abandon the notion that audiences can be taught and moved by irregular or even outlandish images, and he has, significantly, proposed that those elements in the poem which are the agency of delight may be variable and subject to changing times, tastes, and beliefs. But these features of the poem which derive from historical and cultural changes are simply the means of access to something more enduring. Art for Tasso must finally aim at the truth, or, as he puts it in words addressed at the beginning of his third book to Cardinal Aldobrandini, to whom the *Discorsi* are dedicated:

> Many people think, my illustrious lord, that the same thing has happened with the noblest arts and sciences as with peoples, provinces, lands, and oceans, a number of which were not well known to the ancients, but have recently been discovered beyond the Pillars of Hercules to the west, or indeed beyond the altars Alexander set up on the east. They compare the achievements of the poetic and rhetorical arts to the goals and other marks placed as boundaries to timid navigators. But just as I do not blame a daring that is guided by reason, so I do not praise a boldness without reflection, for I think it an insanity that anyone should want

to create an art from chance, virtue from vice, and prudence from temerity, and leave everything to luck, which plays a still smaller role in the workings of the intellectual talent than in the efforts of the body. . . . Still more then ought we to reflect on the workings of the intellect, which always has before it the object itself as the mark it regards: and this is the truth, which never changes or disappears from the mind's eye. But the sign of the Bear disappears to those who, having left behind Abyla and Calpe, sail into the full ocean, although other stars appear in the hemisphere, by which they ought to steer (otherwise they would lack the art of seamanship); and they can somehow manage to elude the sea's inconstancy by the constancy of things celestial. But how much more stable, true, and sure are things intellectual to which we direct the intellect! And even if sometimes we look to things verisimilar, the only notion we can have of them is what our knowledge of truth gives. (P. 57)

Tasso's image for the poet is that of the navigator on uncertain and inconstant seas, and this image is a paradigm for the situation of the reader as well: he must journey with the aid of poetry that caters to his own sense of probability and yet finally draws the mind to verities that have not changed.

VI

Conclusion

In the previous chapters I have looked at bodies of theoretical discourse committed to the proposition that imaginative literature finds both its justification and its formal characteristics through its influence over the audience. Literature is justified first of all by its ability to express moral doctrine and make it plausible. As Scaliger argued, "Imitation . . . is not the end of poetry, but is intermediate to the end. The end is the giving of instruction in pleasurable form, for poetry teaches, and does not simply amuse, as some used to think."[1] Scaliger's statement nicely separates the didactic position in the Renaissance from that of Aristotelians who believed that imitation was indeed the end of poetry and its only distinctive feature. And he suggests also that to pose a purely formal end for poetry is to risk assigning it a largely frivolous cultural function. As to the formal characteristics of the poem, didactic theory tended to place emphasis both on the fiction, which could idealize

169

human experience, and upon those elements of language which were thought capable of reaching the imagination and affections. Such qualities of language are those that stimulate the reader's capacity for internal visualization. The didactic theorist, like the rhetorical theorist, tends to think of language as related to picturing, for what can be "seen" has immediacy and the power to command feeling.

Such properties were important because critics who thought in these terms believed that the task of poetry was to move the will, as well as the reason, towards certain modes of behavior. This bias toward activity as the end of poetry helps explain the interest in faculty psychology, even in the thinking of Dante for whom the purification of the will is a necessary prelude to vision. The proposed moral end and the normative psychology assumed for the audience join to describe that audience as common and largely undifferentiated by culture or historical period. Tasso is the exception here, in part because he seeks an elite audience, at least for the heroic poem, and in part because he accepts verisimilitude as a necessary formal quality in the poem on the grounds that what is verisimilar is more credible. The "miracles" of pre-Christian poetry are not credible in Christian cultures, and by introducing this qualification into a kind of theory where it had not previously been significant, Tasso anticipates one of the central concerns of Neoclassicism. Fracastoro, Barbaro, and Sidney had stressed the vividness and the conceptual perspicuity of the literary image, and in this context no theory of verisimilitude was really necessary. Poetry needed only to be didactically clear and emotionally compelling, and this could well mean that the literary image to be visualized by the reader must be shorn of any historical or other particularities. Tasso's dissent, his insistence on grounding both the heroic poem and its audience in history, marks one of the limits to the mode of didactic theory we have been considering.

Other intellectual forces in the sixteenth and seventeenth centuries also put competitive pressure on this kind of didacticism. First, there is the Neoplatonic interest in contemplative philosophy and literature as transcendent vision; second, there are the efforts to interpret Aristotle's concept of catharsis so as to particularize audiences and, occasionally, to divorce the affective from the intellectual responses of the audience; third, there is a reaction in some quarters of seventeenth century criticism against certain features of Aristotelian faculty psychology. The first two are visible as tendencies in Tasso's *Discourses*; the third heralds an important shift away from confidence in the essentially Humanist view of literature as educating the mind and feelings harmoniously.

In certain rather important respects the Neoplatonic and Humanist concerns are similar. Both believed man capable of rational moderation and a thoughtful knowledge of the good, if only he would not follow the messages of his senses and appetites and thus lose himself in the confused wilderness of material existence. As Herschel Baker has observed, Renaissance Neoplatonism sought to reconcile such tendencies: "The two halves of experience were fused, and natural philosophy, the legitimate domain of secular speculation, proved to be the avenue of the metaphysical."[2] But the direction is toward the metaphysical: "Man, medially situated between spirit and matter, is able through his

active intellect to attain almost deific excellence by sub-
ordinating the baser to the higher element in his complex nature. His highest good is union with God; his
highest knowledge is knowledge of God."[3] Of the
human mind, Ficino maintains that men "have a notion
. . . of intellect itself and of sense, of the intelligible and
of the sensible." Intellect is selfdirected, but without the
guide of reason, sense "is always driven by the instinct
of nature." Yet, asserting that "the nature of mind is
exceedingly spiritual and excellent," he concludes that
"the intellect in its inmost action, frees itself from all
corporeal things. . . . It separates the corporeal forms
from the passions of matter. It also distinguishes from
the corporeal forms those which through their own
natures are completely incorporeal."[4] Although Ficino's
influence on later literature was pervasive, his interest in
esthetic theory was minimal, and the separation he
discusses here is quite contrary to a theory that proposed
the value of literature for the ordinary sensibility. Neoplatonism in its more extended forms sought harmony
of vision in transcendent contemplation. Giordano
Bruno, for example, symbolizing the visionary soul as
Acteon, says, "He sees the Amphitrite, the source of all
numbers, of all species, the monad, the true essence of
the being of all things; and if he does not see it in its own
essence and absolute light, he sees it in its germination
which is similar to it and is its image: for from the
monad, the divinity, proceeds this monad, nature, the
universe, the world. . . .[5] In order to propose such a
transcendence, Bruno has to construct a special psychology: "Understanding, knowledge and vision en-
kindle the desire, and through the ministry of the eyes
the heart becomes enflamed."[6] What Bruno calls sight

has two modes, the intellectual referred to here, and the sensitive; intellectual sight is possible only when the sensitive has been defeated or slain.[7] To poeticize his theories, he creates allegorical poems that he says can only be understood as he dictates and which dramatize a mode of thought which is special, difficult, and arcane.[8] At the outer edges of Renaissance Platonism, then, we encounter a theory of vision which radically divorces sensory and intellectual vision, reserving the latter to certain gifted minds in certain moments. And the result, even for the gifted, is not a reconciliation of the natural and the spiritual, but a version of *contemptus mundi*.

Such speculations are by no means irrelevant to the theories this book has examined. Although they avoid embracing Bruno's kind of visionary art, Fracastoro, Sidney, and Tasso show a close acquaintance with Neoplatonic thought; moreover, a good deal of poetry on the Continent and in England is informed by versions of transcendent contemplation. Henry Reynolds, irritably decrying "forced Art," requires of poets in his own time a rather severe mysticism, and he cannot agree that knowledge of nature and manners is a proper or sufficient subject for poetry.[9] And Thomas Carew, that most secular of the sons of Ben, acknowledges Donne's "holy Rapes upon our Will" and the power of that "brave Soule" who did "the deepe knowledge of dark truths so teach / As sense might judge, what phansie could not reach."[10] In a similar vein George Chapman's aggressive preface to "Hymnus in Noctem" celebrates a difficult path away from ignorance through poetry, and that poem itself praises the obscure symbolisms of non-mimetic fictions.[11] So also his comments on his *Ovid's Banquet of Sense*, in which he "consecrate[s] my strange

Poems to these searching spirits, whom learning hath made noble, and nobilitie sacred. . . ."[12] Such references indicate one of the tendencies to abandon the usual connections between image and idea and to cultivate a sophisticated, erudite readership.

The interest in catharsis, which Hathaway calls "a seminal idea,"[13] moves in quite another direction towards a concentration on the importance of the representation of feelings and passions and from there to a consideration of the quality and significance of the affect experienced by the audience. Here too the tendency is towards increasingly specialized responses, but the specialization is that of the feelings of a broader, more public audience. Some of the critics who deal with the topic are inclined to discount utility in the usual sense that literature is meant to be didactically profitable. Instead—and this is understandable in the case of a direct medium such as drama—there is a decided attack on the Horatian theory of the appeal of literature to the intellect, as Hathaway indicates when he says that "the growth of a purgative theory endangered any broad theory of poetry presupposing that intellect was the general overseer and determiner of all human responses and that even pleasures flowed from assent given to a poetic event by intellective processes capable of creating complex and almost immediate balance sheets, some of which were prudential and some not."[14]

One of the more interesting of the critics who applied himself to the study of catharsis was Agnolo Segni, whose *Ragionamento sopra le Cose Pertinenti alla Poetica* (1573) argues that what Aristotle says about tragedy can be applied to all poetry. But Segni is also a believer in Plato's concept of divine madness as the inspiration of the poet. Hence poetry is essentially irrational, both in its origins and in its effects upon the reader.[15] Poetry is designed to move men, not to satisfy the intellect. Accepting up to a point the kind of psychology with which this book has dealt, Segni differs from didactic critics in refusing to grant that the experience of the senses is a prelude to rational understanding. Sense prompts sensitive appetite only and dwells entirely on appearances.

> Now these powers of our soul being such, poetry, being imitation and fable, consists entirely in appearances, images, and idols, and cannot belong to the intellect, nor be welcomed by it, which seeks the true. But by the other irrational parts it will be received as in its own abode, that is by the appetite through the senses of hearing and sight and through the interior phantasy. And so we affirm that poetry works on the irrational appetite, and that it has for its end not the intellect which finds its truth in the sciences rather than among poets.[16]

Segni, for all this, thinks poetry beneficial because it relieves the feelings. Otherwise his Platonism is orthodox, if elementary. Just as the didactic critic supposes a rational intention on the part of the poet to balance the rational understanding expected of the reader, so Segni on his side is consistent in divorcing both the origin of poetry and its effect from any rational context.

This total, almost Dionysian reduction of poetry to pure affect—allowing poetry as intense an impact as it can manage—was not the major force that altered the view synthesizing sense and intellect, but Segni's ideas do raise the issue of whether poetry has any valid connection at all with philosophical truth. That it does is both the assumption and the argument of the didactic critic in the Renaissance. Segni's negative view is more extreme than Bacon's consignment of poetry to the domain of imagination and opinion, but it foreshadows changes in the seventeenth-century understanding of faculty psychology which in turn were used to support different theories of the relationship between the images of art and the reader's response. This brings us to the third deviation from theories of integrated affect, a deviation sometimes associated with the rise of Baroque art.

The consequence of the speculations of several thinkers, Pallavicino, Peregrini, Tesauro in Italy, and, in England, Hobbes, was the separation of imagination, "fancy" (or phantasy), or "wit" (*ingegno*) from reason or intellect in mental operations. Imagination is thus no longer part of the process by which the mind is able to grasp the true or the real, but instead, almost in the fashion of Plato, the registry of appearances. According to Hobbes, imagination is "decaying sense,"[17] and in dismissal of centuries of received psychological theory he remarks that "Some say the senses receive the species of things, and deliver them to the common sense; and the common sense delivers them over to the fancy, and the fancy to the memory, and the memory to the judgment, like handing of things from one to another, with many words making nothing understood."[18]

The Italians mentioned above put another construction on their divorce of fancy and intellect. Matteo Peregrini's *Delle Acutezze* (1639) sunders "acutezze" (acuteness or wittiness) from systematic thought and makes it entirely a property of style, so that the delight produced by art derives from the artifice of language, not from any relationship the artistic image may have with truth. "In sum," he asserts, "artifice belongs solely or principally not really in discovering beautiful things, but in style; and the object of the probable in our view belongs not to the intellect, which only seeks out the truth and knowledge of things, but indeed to the wit, which insofar as it functions to produce delight has as its object not so much the true as the beautiful."[19] Literature and art, then, are moved away from their kinship with moral philosophy and of course from any didactic end. As audience we are invited to contemplate and take pleasure in the results of the poet's ingenious way with words, and that is offered as a sufficient excuse for the poet's art. Sforza Pallavicino, in *Del Bene* (1644), finds the source of delight in the fable, but the fable is a lie accepted as such by intelligent and learned men. "How then can so corrupted an art be permitted in a Republic of superior men? How can it be praised, and moreover used by holy writers?" The answer is that it offers to the mind so much that is new, marvelous, and splendid that poets have been almost deified. Pallavicino is saying, of course, that the poetic lie offers a rare and special kind of pleasure in explicitly abandoning moral and intellectual benefit as the "soul" of poetry.[20] Instead its justification is in affect: "The more lively the knowledge, the more perfect it is, the more delightful, and the more striking to the appetite."[21] In answer to the objection that such excitation of the passions is harmful, Pallavicino advances the curious explanation that although fearsome artistic images may well move our imagination powerfully and at times fearfully, nevertheless the superior part of our soul remains tranquil.[22]

The cultivation of affect is carried farthest, perhaps, by

Emanuele Tesauro, whose *Cannocchiale Aristotelico* (1655) builds upon Aristotle's *Rhetoric* to explain Marinist poetry by exalting metaphor from a single feature of style into the soul of art. Once again delight is the motive for artifice in a poetic in which, Eugenio Donato says, "the metaphor assumes a completely ornamental value and need no longer bear any relation to conceptual reality."[23] Poets, Tesauro says, like gods, "produce something from nothing: thus from non-being the wit makes being; makes the lion become a man and the eagle [the reference is to the Roman standard] a city."[24] Poetic creation thus becomes arbitrary, destroying the traditional relationship between fiction and reality. Metaphor is ornamental, but ornament carried to the point of creating a new reality with no necessary relationship to truth. The poet's imagination, and perhaps the reader's as well, is autonomous. It might be said that Tesauro realizes the earlier fears as to the consequences of imagination cut loose from its moorings. Marino, the model for Tesauro's concept of metaphor, does precisely what Sidney said the poet must not do: he builds castles in the air. Nor is the poet any longer to be limited in his use of the marvelous as Tasso had urged. Both poet and reader are invited, as Donato suggests, to think of poetry as essentially theatrical, and by implication quite subjective. In theory an audience might no longer be considered universal, or even classifiable by class, culture, or intelligence; rather it could be considered almost infinitely and totally subjective.

It would be quite incorrect to suppose that the Baroque theorists briefly touched upon here represent the dominant critical drift of the seventeenth century. They are of interest in this context to illustrate one of the consequences resulting not so much from an effort to reverse the propositions of the brand of didactic criticism we have examined as from an exaggeration of one of its interests and the nearly total abandonment of another. One sacrifice, in spite of the increased attention to the possible sources of delight, is the concept of a predictable audience.

Such predictability is important to didactic theory in the Renaissance. So long as the poet feigns something like the truth, the reader's response can be plausibly described. An assumption of predictability allows Sidney to mention one ground for preferring poetry to history: "the feigned may be tuned to the highest key of passion . . ." and so move more powerfully than a true example. But intensity apparently can be controlled because the poet has so fashioned his poem that its elements cannot be understood other than as they are intended. Epitomized in Sidney is the assumption of a reader quite a bit more ordinary than Bruno's seeker for high, mysterious, and infinite truth, and whatever else their differences may be, Dante, Fracastoro, Barbaro, Tasso, and Mazzoni also have in view readers common enough. Nor, on the other side, did those many Aristotelians who debated the meaning of *catharsis* envision audiences composed of eccentrics or the mentally ill. And Spenser, that most prominent of English poets to be touched by Neoplatonism, tells Raleigh that he has trimmed his vision to the disposition of those he wishes to reach, and though they are by no means vulgar, they are far from learned: "The generall end therefore of all the booke is to fashion a gentleman or noble person in vertuous and gentle discipline: which for that I conceived shoulde be most plausible and pleasing, being

coloured with an historicall fiction, the which the most
part of men delight to read, rather for variety of matter
than for profit of the ensample."[25] His concession to an
audience is ancient and conventional: he knows that if
he would influence his audience he must provide food
for their fancies. This fancy is neither drastically visionary nor totally sensory. It is delighted by appearances,
and though there may be too great an interest in variety
of matter, we are to understand that the gentleman may
be identified nevertheless.

Even though such apparently mundane intentions
directed at mundane audiences may seem tedious or in
some respects at odds with Sidney's images of improvement on nature or Fracastoro's simple universal idea in
all its beauty, they register the hopeful attempt of poets
to bring important truth and the more or less ordinary
mind together. In somewhat different terms it might be
said that the proposed task of the poet is to join intellect
and feeling to influence behavior. The hierarchies in
which post-classical philosophy arranged the universe
and the soul were viewed as a kind of unity, and, as we
have seen, Neoplatonism proposed a doctrine of ideas as
an especially dominant unity of being, but one which
tended to reinforce the view that everything ordinarily
attributable to the human consciousness—appetite, perception, feeling, judgment, discursive reasoning, will—
could only be valid when directed beyond, as well as at,
the immediate objects of that consciousness. For an
extremist such as Bruno that goal was an infinity, and he
proposed a kind of intellectual rapture or frenzy as the
energy to keep the soul pointed in that direction.

For the mainstream of critical theory it was understood that readers had to be approached more on their

own terms. Epistemology might lead man beyond his senses and the feelings they and his imagination provoke, but it certainly begins there. This was the inherited lesson of the schools of rhetoric, and the theorists we have examined, including Dante, and including those who abandon teaching as a goal of poetry, were more than usually conscious of the notions of persuasion and moving attached to rhetoric. The most persistent aim of poetry was understood to be an influence over audience behavior, and as we have seen there is very little confidence that behavior can be manipulated by an appeal to reason alone: the feeling part of man, so conventional doctrine runs, must be subordinated to reason and a properly instructed will, but the feeling part cannot be left to chance. Men share the gift of intelligence with angels, but angels do not share the burden of flesh and sense.

Though Dante holds the general psychological theories of his successors in the Renaissance, his notion of how art may benefit the observer necessarily differs quite markedly. The issue is not something like Sidney's architectonic knowledge but such knowledge of self and the universe as will lead to union with God. The truth to be acquired has a serial, sequential, and hierarchical order, leading from the more to the less obvious. Moreover, the *Commedia* is unusual in that the act of knowing is part of the fiction of the poem. At the same time, Dante's emphasis upon the education of the will, in part through the artistic schooling of the senses and appetites, provides a continuity with later Humanist interests in the power of language to reach and harmonize the faculties of the soul. We see this in Salutati, and we see in him also a wider tolerance of antique and secular literature. Fracastoro is even more liberal in his conception of what poetry can teach, and like Barbaro he attends closely to the poet's and reader's capacity to move from image to idea. In their different fashions Sidney and Tasso prolong this tradition, exploring the ways in which poetry, as a branch of moral philosophy, may delight and move the reader and at the same time direct him to "practical" knowledge. The Renaissance theorists of didacticism urge a union of compelling beauty and worthy doctrine, significance made lovely and loveliness made significant. For they believed that they had found an answer to Plato's doubts about poetry in the artist's capacity to set doctrine before our eyes—in her holiday apparel, as Sidney says—to touch and control the common responsive powers of imagination, feeling, and will. These are powers that may be tuned to good or ill. They are as unstable as human life, but in the eyes of these critics they are charged with possibility and scarcely limited, if at all, by time, culture, or the constraints of individual temperament.

But if poetry has such power to move the imagination and will, some means must be found to guarantee its moral value. The older answer to this problem was the resource of allegorical interpretation, but by Sidney's time this had ceased to be sufficient to justify any and all forms of fiction. For different reasons neither he nor Tasso is willing to accept all forms of the fabulous, and in following their arguments we can observe the theoretical tradition concerned with poetry as a moving and teaching instrument beginning to narrow its tolerance of certain kinds of poetic invention. We can notice in them, and even in Mazzoni, subtle shifts back and forth between descriptive and prescriptive criticism, acknowledging on the one hand the poet's freedom and the value of this and on the other hand insisting upon the presence of sound doctrine or verisimilitude or both. There is simply no room in didactic theory for a view of art which proceeds from a sense of its utter independence. We have instead theories that in varying degrees attempt to define art according to its special nature as a form of discourse (revealing and conveying those dimensions of reality and ideality that history and philosophy alone do not) and according to traditional notions of the mental capacities of the audience.

The latter is the dominant motive of sixteenth century didacticism, and critics in that tradition are constrained to judge poetic form primarily according to its persuasive effectiveness. In other words, the reader's mind must be susceptible to an internal and vivid perception of the literary image, and the image must be such that he understands the concept it embodies in such a way that his behavior is thereby influenced. This process is exemplified by Dante's response to the graven images on the terrace of pride and by Sidney's and Tasso's reading of the figure of Aeneas: the reader must grasp the point of such images—their "essence" to borrow the jargon of the times—and that point is not their resemblance to historical figures nor even their artificial excellence (though this is necessary), but rather their moral character. This does not mean that there is to be no resemblance of any kind to nature or experience; some connection must be made, though where allegory is tolerated, such resemblance may be slight. Verisimilitude, most vigorously insisted upon by Tasso, exists largely for the sake of attracting the reader, but that attraction is made more powerful still by heightening, by improving on nature in some way, either through the agency of ornament, as Fracastoro would have it, or through Sidney's picture of a golden world, or by means of the marvelous.[26]

With the Baroque theorists we may wonder, at this point, whether some power higher than the imagination is required of the reader. Tasso somewhat tentatively proposes the visionary phantasy in talking of the poet's powers, and also requires it of the reader, but in general that aspect of thought which can absorb example and give significance to the images present in the imagination was regarded as sufficient. This may mean another implicit limitation upon the kind of poetry allowed into the canon: images so cryptic and abstruse as Bruno's are unintelligible to the common reader or they require the author's prose interpretation. We have already observed that the poet is expected to modify his images according to conceptual requirements and the necessity of giving pleasure; he must also choose them so that they may be read properly. At times this might mean that the author would moralize his own work. In any case, the spirit of rationalism which Humanists sought to adjust to the requirements of moving became increasingly powerful in the seventeenth century, in one form of critical theory at least, and led to a very different understanding of the connections of poetry to human faculties. Imagination, to return to Hobbes, is nothing but decaying sense, not an aid to both a feeling and intellectual response to art. The critics whom I have examined sought to locate poetry in both the universe of thought and the experience of sense, imagination, and feeling. But for Hobbes, and for others like him, it seemed much more mundane, submitting the faculties to a different balance and deriving its form from custom and experience in the world:

> Time and Education begets experience; Experience begets Memory; Memory begets Judgment and Fancy: Judgment begets the strength and structure, and fancy begets the ornaments of a Poem.[27]

For Hobbes, writing in 1650, fancy is the faculty of discovering resemblances and judgment is the means for discovering differences and making distinctions. With this division of labor, the effort to harmonize the faculties and balance the claims of sense and intellect and will is gone.

Notes

INTRODUCTION

1. To take three examples at random, such is the case in Joel Spingarn, *A History of Literary Criticism in the Renaissance*; J. W. Atkins, *English Literary Criticism: The Renascence*; and the comprehensive survey by William K. Wimsatt, Jr., and Cleanth Brooks, *Literary Criticism: A Short History*. It is not that scholars in the twentieth century have been unaware of earlier efforts to propose theories of audience response. Instead they have found other questions in the history of literary theory more compelling, possibly because generalizations about the audience are virtually impossible to verify. There are no texts to refer to. One may also mention the modern influence of the views of Monroe Beardsley and William K. Wimsatt, Jr. in "The Affective Fallacy," in which they deride the heresy of "judging a poem by its *results*" (*The Verbal Icon*, p. 21). However, a recent article points to a change in mood, at least insofar as post-Renaissance theory is concerned: see Robert DeMaria, Jr., "The Ideal Reader: A Critical Fiction," especially the bibliography on p. 473 n. 1.

2. Cf. Plotinus, "On the Intellectual Beauty," *The Enneads*, Eighth Tractate, Fifth Ennead; Longinus, *On The Sublime*,

especially Section XV on images, pp. 86–88; and Proclus, "Proclus on the More Difficult Questions in the *Republic*: The nature of Poetic Art," trans. Thomas Taylor, rev. Kevin Kerrane in Alex Preminger, O. B. Hardison, Jr., Kevin Kerrane, eds., *Classical and Medieval Literary Criticism: Translations and Interpretations*, pp. 313–315.

3. I refer to certain general tendencies remarked by P. O. Kristeller when he says that Renaissance Humanism was "a cultural and educational program which emphasized and developed an important but limited area of studies"; "The Humanist Movement," in *Renaissance Thought: The Classic, Scholastic, and Humanistic Strains*, p. 11. Kristeller's emphasis on the literary and rhetorical preoccupations of Humanism is echoed by Hanna Gray, "Renaissance Humanism: The Pursuit of Eloquence," *JHI* 24 (1963): 497–514, who connects the interest in eloquence with the valuing of the active life, and by Nancy Streuver, *The Language of History in the Renaissance: Rhetoric and Historical Consciousness in Florentine Humanism*. See esp. p. 67: ". . . rhetorical analysis made the Humanists sensitive to the affective aspects of language; the concern with figure and sound is conducive to the inclusion of irrational as well as rational aspects of thought in the reconstruction of the past, of thought-as-experience."

4. Murray W. Bundy, *The Theory of Imagination in Classical and Medieval Thought*; Baxter Hathaway, *The Age of Criticism: The Late Renaissance in Italy*, Part Four: "The Poetic Imagination." Both works are indispensable to any study of pre-seventeenth-century theory in its references to psychology.

5. Isabel G. MacCaffrey, *Spenser's Allegory: The Anatomy of Imagination*, pp. 13–32.

6. Cf. O. B. Hardison, Jr., *The Enduring Monument: A Study of the Idea of Praise in Renaissance Literary Theory and Practice*, Chaps. I and III; also Preminger, Hardison, Kerrane, eds., *Classical and Medieval Literary Criticism*, pp. 270–275. The following sections of Cicero's *De Oratore* are especially suggestive: I. v. 17–19 (the importance of the emotions of the audience); I. xii. 52–xiii. 55 (the poet is kinsman to the orator); III. vii 25–viii. 31 (the arts and pleasure); II. i. 195–197 (the naturally affective power of words).

7. Those interested in the ways in which poetry was severally classified in relation to other disciplines in the Middle Ages and Renaissance should consult Bernard Weinberg, *A History of Literary Criticism in the Italian Renaissance*, I, 1–137; Hardison, *The Enduring Monument*, pp. 3–23; and, for an exhaustive study of the interdependence of oratorical and literary theory in antiquity, the following essays by Wesley Trimpi: "The Ancient Hypothesis of Fiction: An Essay on the Origins of Literary Theory," and "The Quality of Fiction: The Rhetorical Transmission of Literary Theory."

8. Giovanni Boccaccio, *Genealogia Deorum Gentilium*, Preface and Books XIV and XV; trans. as *Boccaccio on Poetry*, XIV. vii (p. 39).

9. Preminger, Hardison, Kerrane, eds., *Classical and Medieval Literary Criticism*, p. 276.

10. *Boccaccio on Poetry*, XIV. ix (p. 51).

11. Ibid., XIV. xii (p. 59).

12. Michael Murrin, *The Veil of Allegory: Some Notes Toward a Theory of Allegorical Rhetoric in the English Renaissance*, p. 13.

13. *The Enduring Monument*, p. 63.

14. Ibid., pp. 54–67. These pages are an excellent discussion of the importance of example in didactic literary theory.

15. Spenser's letter to Raleigh prefacing *The Faerie Queene*. Murrin, pp. 98–166, reads Spenser as aiming at an elite and specialized audience, in effect an audience of critics.

I: FACULTY PSYCHOLOGY AND THEORIES OF IMAGINATION

1. *The Institutio Oratorio*, I, 323.

2. *Nichomachaean Ethics*, Bk. II. Moral virtue "is concerned with passions and actions . . ." (1106b). My text for this work and *De Anima* is *The Basic Works of Aristotle*. References to these works are in the text.

3. See below, pp. 24–25.

4. Aristotle's general concept of mind may be represented by this statement: "Now mind is one and continuous in the sense in which the process of thinking is so, and thinking is identical with the thoughts which are its parts; these have a

serial unity like that of number, not a unity like that of a spatial magnitude" (407a).

5. *De Somniis* 460b, trans. J. I. Beare in *The Works of Aristotle.*

6. *De Memoria et Reminiscentia* 450b, trans. J. I. Beare in *The Works of Aristotle.*

7. *De Rhetorica* 1370a–1370b, trans. W. Rhys Roberts in *The Works of Aristotle.*

8. Aristotle postulates two modes of the intellect: the contemplative, which is without movement and which he says can regard a painting without affect; and the practical, which he associates with appetite because it leads to action.

9. In *De Memoria et Reminiscentia* 450a, Aristotle mentions the abstract imagining of temporal and spatial dimensions. He insists, however, that this form of imagining, associated with the memory of intellectual objects, requires "presentation" in the mind through the *sensus communis*, the faculty that combines images or impressions from the several senses into wholes. This mental process "belongs to the faculty of intelligence only incidentally, while directly and essentially it belongs to the primary faculty of sense perception."

10. *Republic* VI, 509–511. The text is *The Dialogues of Plato*, trans. Benjamin Jowett. Just before this excerpt is the comparison of clear knowledge with the sun's illumination of the sense of sight (508), an analogy used by Aristotle and Augustine, among many others.

The passage I quote, which concludes Book VI, has been variously translated, and there has been some objection to Jowett's term "faculties" for *pathemata*. Shorey in the Loeb edition uses "affections," while Cornford has "states of mind." Instead of Jowett's "perception of shadows" for "eikasia," Shorey writes "picture-thinking" and Cornford "imagining." Strictly speaking, Plato is discussing modes of thinking related to the categories of objects of thought; faculties of mind are implied. Cf. Plato, *The Republic*, trans. Paul Shorey, II, 116–117; and *The Republic of Plato*, trans. F. M. Cornford, p. 226.

11. This division of types of imitation was adapted and substantially modified by Jacopo Mazzoni, *On the Defense of the*

Comedy of Dante, p. 13. Mazzoni considers icastic imitation the representation of things that exist or are thought to exist, and phantastic the representation of that which the poet or artist believes he has made up in his own imagination. Where Plato consigns all literature and art to the realm of the phantastic, Mazzoni thinks them capable of both kinds of representation and uses the icastic-phantastic distinction as a way of categorizing genres.

12. For example, Bundy in *The Theory of Imagination in Classical and Medieval Thought*, p. 30: "The charge against the painter—and the sculptor and the dramatist—is that through phantasy they become subjective artists. Not only are they concerned with material objects rather than with ideas, but they insist upon reproducing this material world from their peculiar points of view. Imagination leads the artist to deal with the material, the changing, the objects of opinion. Phantasy leads him to an error still more serious: to deal with the individual and the relative."

Bundy's extensive survey of classical and medieval thinking about imagination is a search for evidence in these periods of some theory of creative artistic power, a search that is largely disappointed by the general consignment of imagination to the lower powers of the soul; nevertheless his study is valuable to anyone concerned with psychological theory and its relation to art and literature prior to the Renaissance.

13. Preminger, Hardison, Kerrane, eds., *Classical and Medieval Literary Criticism*, p. 313.

14. Ibid., pp. 313–315.

15. *On Christian Doctrine*, p. 10.

16. *The Enneads*, III. 6–7 (pp. 208–209). For a comparison of the two systems, see Ronald H. Nash, *The Light of the Mind: St. Augustine's Theory of Knowledge*, pp. 4–5.

17. *De Genesi ad Litteram*, XII. vii (p. 388).

18. Cf. Nash, *The Light of the Mind*, p. 7, and Rudolph Allers, "St. Augustine's Doctrine on Illumination," pp. 40–41.

19. *The Enneads*, IV. 2. 1.

20. *The Trinity*, trans. Stephen MacKenna, *The Fathers of the Church*, XI.2 (p. 317).

21. I am referring to *The Trinity*, IX–XIII.

22. The following passage suggests a fundamental difference from Aristotle's organic notion of universals: "For it is not by seeing many minds with our bodily eyes that we gather, by way of analogy, a general or special knowledge of the human mind; but we contemplate the inviolable truth, whence we can as perfectly as possible define, not what each man's mind is, but what it ought to be in the light of eternal types" (*The Trinity*, IX.6 [p. 279]).

23. Ibid.

24. Ibid., p. 281.

25. Ibid., pp. 281–282.

26. *De Genesi ad Litteram*, XII. 9 (p. 391).

27. *On Christian Doctrine*, p. 37.

28. *The Trinity*, XI. 4 (p. 325).

29. *De Anima* 433a–433b. Aristotle states that the faculty of appetite is what originates movement: "As it is, mind is never found producing movement without appetite (for wish is a form of appetite; and when movement is produced according to calculation it is also according to wish), but appetite can originate movement contrary to calculation, for desire is a form of appetite" (433a). Again, " . . . it follows that while that which originates movement must be specifically one, viz. the faculty of appetite as such (or rather farthest back of all the object of that faculty; for it is it that itself remaining unmoved originates the movement by being apprehended in thought or imagination), the things that originate movement are numerically many" (433b). He has also noted that "the mind is capable of receiving an object" (429a). Generally Aristotle requires either the presence of objects to be sensed or images to be imagined before the processes of appetite and thought may occur, so that even though the mind is capable of thinking itself (429b–430a), appetite and thought are reflexive powers initially.

Augustine is somewhat more emphatic than Aristotle in believing that the imagination may possess a greater clarity and intensity than ordinary sensory vision, especially when desire or fear are strong, or when the balance of the soul is disturbed by sickness or dreams. But he does not explain satisfactorily what it is that first moves the will to concentrate on one thing rather than another. His greater emphasis on the power of affect derived from imagined things no doubt has something to do with his reaction against worldliness; see *The Trinity*, XI. 6 (p. 326). In any case, he appears to believe that the explanation is to be found in the mind, rather than in any quality of the perceived object or image: see *The Trinity*, VIII. 3 (p. 248) and IX. 6 (p. 279). It has sometimes been suggested that Augustine anticipates the doctrine of innate ideas; see F. L. Copleston, *A History of Medieval Philosophy*, p. 35; Nash, *The Light of the Mind*, pp. 57—59; and Allers, "St. Augustine's Doctrine on Illumination," pp. 38—39.

30. *The Trinity*, XI. 6 (p. 326). Plotinus has a rather different view of the relationship of volition and imagination: "Taking it that the presentment of fancy is not a matter of our will and choice, how can we think those acting at its dictation to be free agents? Fancy, strictly, in our use, takes its rise from conditions of the body; . . . We refuse to range under the principle of freedom those whose conduct is directed by such fancy. . . . Self-disposal, to us, belongs to those who, through the activities of the Intellectual-Principle, live above the states of the body" (*The Enneads*, VI. 8. 3 [p. 597]).

31. *The Trinity*, VIII. 3 (pp. 247—248).

32. Ibid., p. 248.

33. Cf. Nash, *The Light of the Mind*, p. 81.

34. Augustine, *Letters*, No. 7, pp. 16—17.

35. Aquinas, *Summa Theologiae*, vol. 12, trans. Paul T. Durbin (London, 1963), Ia. 84. 5. My references to the *Summa Theologiae* are to this series. A detailed survey of the views of Aquinas may be found in E. Ruth Harvey, *The Inward Wits: Psychological Theory in the Middle Ages and the Renaissance*, pp. 52—61.

36. Etienne Gilson summarizes Aquinas' views as follows: "We must . . . attribute to the intellect an active virtue which renders the intelligible, contained potentially in sensible reality, actually intelligible; and this virtue has been called 'intellectus agens,' or the active intellect" (*The Philosophy of St. Thomas Aquinas*, p. 191).

37. *S.T.*, Ia. 78. 4. Aquinas disagrees pointedly with Averroes and Avicenna, who considered that there were two

separate imaginative faculties, one reproductive and the other formative; cf. F. Rahman, *Avicenna's Psychology*, pp. 30−39. Albertus Magnus follows the Arabic view in enumerating the powers of the soul; there are, in his account, the *common sense*, which sorts out magnitude, form, number, stillness, and motion; the *imagination*, which receives sense impressions already processed by the common sense and reproduces them as images for the use of the higher or rational "virtues"; the *estimative power*, which elicits "intentions" not accessible to the exterior senses (friendliness, hostility, fidelity, sociability, etc.); the *phantasy proper*, which studies the particulars to be reasoned about and combines and divides images and intentions; the *appetites*, which are both intellective (i.e. the will) and sensitive; and the *intellect*, which consists in the possible or potential intellect and the active, whose function is to abstract the image so as to offer its universal status to the possible intellect. I have drawn this schematic summary from a late fifteenth-century version of Albertus's several treatises on the soul, *Textus Triorum Libriorum De Anima Aristotelis cum Commentario Doctrinas Veneralibus Domini Alberti Magni*, sig. riii−riii^V. In Chaps. 13−15 of *De Anima* Albertus discusses the "apprehensive" powers of the sensitive soul. *Imaginatione* designates a receptacle for images drawn from the common sense; it is a term merely describing the place where images appear. On the other hand, *imaginativa* is associated with the terms *cogitativa* and *formativa*; it too has a location, in the middle cavity of the brain. The several terms designate several principles of mental function: when the intellect is governing, the power is *cogitativa* or an ordering function; when the sensitive soul is governing, the power is *imaginativa*; when the mind is occupied with combining or dividing images, the proper term is *formativa*. The latter mode, according to Albertus, is equivalent to building castles in the air or imagining chimeras. *De Anima*, as well as a companion treatise, *De Apprehensione*, may be found in a modern edition, Vol. 5 of *Opera Omnia*.

It is interesting to note that, although compared to those of Augustine Albertus's categories are terminologically more precise, and his interest in the location of faculties in the head quite pronounced, nevertheless he ascribes multiple functions to the same faculty and seems to regard both "imaginative" powers as functions of the sensitive soul. The suggestion of Bundy, pp. 255–256, *et passim*, that the phantasy was sometimes considered a faculty of the rational soul has to be approached with some caution in respect to the writings of Albertus and many other medieval comments on psychology.

38. Another distinction appears if we compare the systems of Aquinas and Duns Scotus. Taking the example of the way in which we have knowledge of ourselves, Copleston says, "The difference between Scotus and St. Thomas concerns, then, the explanation of a fact, rather than the fact itself. Both agree that the soul is actually without an immediate intuition of itself in this life; but, whereas St. Thomas explains this fact in terms of the nature of the human soul, attacking the Platonist view of the relation of soul to body, Scotus . . . explains it in terms of a hindrance, even suggesting that this hindrance may be due to sin and quoting St. Augustine in support of his suggestion" (*A History of Philosophy:* vol. 2, *Mediaeval Philosophy: Augustine to Scotus*, p. 491). See *S.T.* Ia. 88. 3.

Aquinas should also be contrasted with Avicenna, who did not believe that a material image was required for a knowledge of universals. Harvey, *The Inward Wits*, p. 58, explains: "Aquinas asserts that in contemplating the universal 'man' or 'horse' the intellect always has before it some mental image or phantasm of a single man or horse as it has been perceived through the senses. The phantasm necessarily has some of the limitations of a real individual horse, but the intellect considers it as an example of its species, and ignores as far as possible its individual features. This theory places the intellect in much closer collaboration with the body."

39. *De Genesi ad Litteram*, XII. 9 (p. 391).

40. *Aristotle's* De Anima *in the Version of William of Moerbeke and the Commentary of St. Thomas Aquinas*, p. 399.

41. Ibid.

42. Ibid. The Latin reads, "*sed etiam formare imaginativae virtutis phantasmata*," which this edition translates, "and also make up the forms of fancy." More literally it can be rendered,

"but even to form the phantasms of the imaginative power." Though considered a power of the sensitive soul, the imagination can be commanded by the intellect to create images or phantasms.

43. *The Theory of Imagination in Classical and Medieval Thought*, pp. 277–278.

44. An idea of the dominant position of Aristotelian psychology in the Renaissance can be gained by a glance at Hermann Schüling, *Bibliographie der Psychologischen Literatur des. 16 Jahrhunderts*. Schüling's index lists sixty-one editions of and/or commentaries on *De Anima* alone, including some in multiple editions. These are in addition to works derived in one way or another from Aristotle.

45. *On the Imagination: The Latin Text with an Introduction, and English Translation, and Notes*. This Pico is the nephew of the more famous Platonist. His treatise is in part a recension of Scholastic psychology and seeks to return to what Pico believes is the simpler scheme of Aristotle. Its emphasis is on the dangers of imagination and on practical methods to avoid them. At the same time, Pico gives the imagination a central role in human consciousness and behavior (p. 39) and provides a traditional description of its various powers (p. 29). Furthermore, he concedes that with the aid of faith, appeals to the imagination of the reader can be useful (p. 91). What is largely suspect to the stern Christian moralist (Pico was a follower of Savanarola) is exactly what recommends imagination to the literary critic: its emotional strength and vividness. For an account of these divided attitudes in sixteenth-century England, see William Rossky, "Imagination in the English Renaissance: Psychology and Poetic," pp. 49–73.

46. There is a useful summary of the influence of Aristotelian and Scholastic psychology on sixteenth-century concepts of the passions in Anthony Levi, *French Moralists: The Theory of the Passions, 1585 to 1649*, chap. 2.

47. See Juan Luis Vives, *De Anima et Vita*, pp. 146–147, and Levi's discussion, pp. 25–27. Vives's text may also be found in *Opera Omnia*. Vives reflects the Stoic variation from Aristotle in combining phantasy and judgment into a single faculty that creates monstrous or marvelous images, guesses at the future,

and assists in discerning the true from the false (*Opera Omnia*, III, 326–328).

48. In this summary of Salutati's thought, I follow Charles Trinkaus, *In Our Image and Likeness: Humanity and Divinity in Italian Humanist Thought*, I 147.

49. Ibid., I, 63–64.

50. Coluccio Salutati, *De Laboribus Herculis*, I, 68.

51. *Epistolario di Coluccio Salutati*, Letter XIII, to Fra Giovanni da Samminiato, IV, 177. The translation is that of Trinkaus.

52. Ibid., Letter XXIV, to Fra Giovanni, IV, 230.

53. Ibid., IV, 231.

II: DANTE'S ESTHETIC OF GRACE AND THE READER'S IMAGINATION

1. *De Vulgari Eloquentia*, I, iii.

2. *Convivio*, III, iii.

3. Ibid., III, ii. Busnelli and Vandelli, the editors of the Le Monnier edition (Firenze, 1968), cite Aquinas's *Summa Contra Gentiles* as the primary text by which to gloss this passage and its surrounding context. For example, Aquinas says, "Now, sensible things cannot lead the human intellect to the point of seeing in them the nature of divine substance; for sensible things are effects that fall short of the power of their cause. Yet, beginning with sensible things, our intellect is led to the point of knowing about God that He exists, and other such characteristics that must be attributed to the First Principle" (*Summa Contra Gentiles*, I. 3, 3). Additionally: "In this faith there are truths preached that surpass every human intellect; the pleasures of the flesh are curbed; it is taught that the things of the world should be spurned. Now, for the minds of mortal men to assent to these things is the greatest of miracles, just as it is a manifest work of divine inspiration that, spurning visible things, men should seek only what is invisible" (I. 6, 1). At the same time Dante's reference to the intellect being "divested of matter" might also be referred to Augustine's concept of intellectual vision, the possession of *rationes aeternae* by faith rather than through a process of deliberation involving sense images and sequential thought. CF. *The Trinity*,

Book III and *De Genesi ad Litteram*, Book XII.

4. *Convivio*, III, iv.

5. This is the position of Bundy, pp. 225–256.

6. *Epistolae*, X, p. 351.

7. This and subsequent translations of passages from the *Vita Nuova* are Mark Musa's in *Dante's Vita Nuova: A Translation and an Essay*.

8. The several spirits were thought to be rarefied substances that linked the soul to bodily organs. The vital spirit is formed in the heart from purified blood and is responsible for the passions. The natural spirit, derived from the liver, allows each part of the body to draw its proper nourishment. The animal spirit, composed of the vital spirit and air, provides the powers of reason, sensation, and motion. Cf. Harvey, *The Inward Wits*, pp. 1–30.

This passage from the *Vita Nuova* should be understood with certain qualifications: Dante is only nine years old at his first encounter with Beatrice. Musa, in *Dante's Vita Nuova*, pp. 168–173, suggests that it is an ironic or mocking account of youthful "folly" by the more mature poet, but this need not divert us from the seriousness of the experience. Certainly the description of affect is straightforward enough. General summaries of Dante's psychology may be found in Philip H. Wicksteed, *Dante and Aquinas*, pp. 153–186, and T. K. Swing, *The Fragile Leaves of the Sibyl: Dante's Master Plan*, pp. 29–76. The latter proposes to coordinate a systematic doctrine of the nature of the soul with the structure of the *Commedia*.

9. On the significance of this term, see C. S. Singleton, *An Essay on the "Vita Nuova,"* pp. 25–54.

10. In one account of the effects of Beatrice's voice and eyes the image fades in the mind of the beholder because it is too miraculous: according to the last lines of the lyric in Chapter 21, "non si po dicer ne tener a mente / Si é novo miracolo a gentile." Compare this with Dante's remarks at the beginning of the *Paradiso* on the failure of his memory to recall everything he witnessed in the heavens.

11. For example, Bundy, *The Theory of Imagination in Classical and Mediaeval Thought*, pp. 227–228, sees Dante's presentation as "typical of the descriptive psychology of the Middle Ages"

and offering an account of "wrong opinions . . . dangerous passions . . . wrong physical states." Bundy's limited reading of this aspect of the work seems to derive from his failure to find in it a "theory of mystical vision," a higher poetic of the creative imagination which he discovers in the *Paradiso*.

12. The significance of the dream is complex. It has strong religious overtones and marks a transition in Dante's emotions from carnal to spiritual love. See Singleton, *An Essay on the Vita Nuova*, pp. 56–57. Singleton's view of the work as an allegory of the growth of spiritual love should be compared to Musa's argument that it is a contest between profane and sacred love in the protagonist's mind.

13. In addition to the usual belief that Dante is recalling *De Anima*, III, one should consider *Ethica Nichomachea*, VI, 1142^b–1143^b, where Aristotle distinguishes between speculative and practical reasoning and mentions understanding and judgment, but not imagination, as features of the practical intellect. Dante's term *inventiva* may correspond to Aristotle's "art" or "the capacity to make," which is one of the five powers of the rational intellect, "the states by virtue of which the soul possesses truth by way of affirmation or denial" (*E.N.*, 1139^{b}3). Here imagination and reason would seem to be conflated, at least for the purpose of certain kinds of mental activity.

14. Singleton's notes to this section in his *Purgatorio*, Part II, pp. 355–356, cite Bonaventure, Aquinas, and *De Monarchia* on the doctrine of free will to which Dante refers.

15. "You see well, reader, that I uplift my theme: do not wonder, therefore, if I sustain it with greater art" (11. 70–72). Landino comments that Dante asks the reader not to wonder if "more than is usual adorns his poem with various figures in this place, showing that the elevation of the material demands it" (*Dante con l'Espositione . . . de . . . Landino*, p. 196. The translation here and for Vellutello below is mine.) Vellutello draws an analogy to architecture: the higher a building, the stronger must be its structure. The same is true in writing, "because the material, which he wishes to treat, is elevated in its style, so it has a greater need to be fortified with art if it is to be sustained." Vellutello's commentary immediately follows

that of Landino in this edition of the *Commedia*.

16. Whether or not the mind could know God and how, had attracted various speculation. At one side of the question is Bonaventure, whose thought is in some respects like Dante's, but in *The Mind's Road to God*, p. 8, his rationalism specifically excludes the imagination from the process of approaching knowledge of God through His "traces" in nature. Cf. Copleston, *A History of Philosophy*, II, 290. The view supplied by Arabic philosophy locates a power of phantasy in the rational soul, separate from the sensitive imagination and able to leap beyond the mind's experience of material nature. Cf. chapter one, n. 33, above. The position of Aquinas, which Dante appears to share, avoids both the denial that the "lower" faculties must be suspended and the view that requires a rational phantasy to suit a special object of knowledge. First, in arguing against Avicenna's notion of the rational phantasy, Aquinas notes that only men can combine images of actual objects to fabricate new wholes: "But this activity is not found in animals other than man, in whom the power of imagination suffices to account for it" (*S.T.* Ia. 78. 4). Then, concerning our power to derive universals from particular objects, he says, "Our intellect both abstracts species from sense images—in so far as it considers the natures of things as universal—and yet, at the same time, understands these in sense images, since it cannot understand even the things from which it abstracts species without turning to sense images . . ." (*S.T.* Ia. 85. 1). As regards the knowledge of spiritual realities, he follows Aristotle in asserting that "we cannot, primarily and essentially, in the mode of knowing that we experience, understand immaterial substances since they are not subject to the senses and imagination." However, "We can rise from material things to a knowledge of immaterial things, but not to a perfect knowledge because there is not a sufficient proportion between material and immaterial realities" (*S.T.* Ia. 88. 2). For Aquinas the question is not one of absolute knowledge of God as he really is, but an imperfect mode of knowledge based on the inference that there must be a kind of correspondence between the material and the immaterial: "Thus we must say simply that God is not the first

thing known by us. Rather, we arrive at a knowledge of God, by way of creatures, as St. Paul says, *The invisible things of God are there for the mind to see in the things He has made. . . .* We understand and judge all things in the light of the first truth because the light of our intellect, whether natural or the gift of grace, is nothing more than an image of the first truth . . ." (*S.T.* Ia. 88. 3). A poet such as Dante may not only look to a theory of knowledge of this kind as part of his theology but also incorporate it as one of the central themes of his work: it is evident, I think, that the effort of the pilgrim to acquire knowledge dramatizes the experience of the senses, the imagination, and the reason, acknowledging also the powers and limitations of each. For a brief account of the fashion in which Dante responds to disparate theological temperaments and for his qualified attraction to mystical thought, see Thomas Bergin, *Dante*, pp. 63–65.

17. Bundy, *The Theory of Imagination in Classical and Mediaeval Thought*, pp. 236–237.

18. For example, Albertus Magnus, whose *De Apprehensione* Bundy cites (pp. 370–372) as representative of this tradition. Bundy is interested in Dante's references to imaginative experience as evidence of a theory of artistic creation, but the visions the *Commedia* dramatizes and the psychology Dante records with such particularity are those of the spectator, not the artist. In fairness I should note that at least one Renaissance editor, Bernardo Daniello, supposes that the vision in *Purgatorio* 17 takes place in the phantasy, not the imagination. Cf. *Dante con l'Espositione di . . . Daniello*, p. 353.

19. My text is C. S. Singleton's translation, *The Divine Comedy: Purgatorio*.

20. Dante's delighted absorption in these carvings, which are "for their Craftsman's sake precious to behold," must only last briefly, lest he be diverted from his upward progress. Virgil gently informs him that "many people" have arrived on the terrace and will "direct us on to the high stairs" (11. 100–102). By this transition Dante offers a soft reminder that art, however instructive and delightful, is only a means to an end.

21. In Canto 13 there is a similar scene, the encounter with those who expiate envy by going about with their eyelids wired shut.

22. Singleton's note to line 26 (*Purgatorio*, II, 451–452) refers us to Marco Lombardo's discourse on the innate power of moral discrimination. See also C. S. Singleton, *Dante Studies II: Journey to Beatrice*, p. 30.

23. Francis X. Newman, "St. Augustine's Three Visions and the Structure of the *Commedia*," p. 59. Singleton refers mainly to Aquinas for an understanding of the three levels of vision; see *Dante Studies II: Journey to Beatrice*, pp. 15–34.

24. Newman, p. 69.

25. See, for example, the discourses in Cantos 16–18 and 25.

26. Singleton, *Dante Studies II: Journey to Beatrice*, p. 115, analyzes the dream as follows: "If Leah is the desire for justice and justice resides in the will, then it must be that Virgil leads to Leah Outside the dream, in the event of the poem, there is no figure to represent her. . . . She is the perfection of the active life, she is justice and from her the wayfarer can pass to her sister Rachel, that is, to contemplation. Leah is the disposition for the higher life beyond. First justice, then contemplation."

27. I refer the reader to Singleton's *Dante Studies II* for a comprehensive reading. See especially Part II, "Return to Eden."

28. My text is Singleton's translation.

29. Marguerite Mills Chiarenza, "The Imageless Vision and Dante's *Paradiso*." For a different understanding of the *Paradiso* and especially of the vision at its end, see Dennis John Costa, "Dante as a Poet-Theologian." Costa thinks of Canto 33, ll. 125–132, the circles of light which appeared to Dante to be "painted in our effigy," as "an intuition of the Incarnation as Trinitarian mystery . . . the revealed Logos and his role in salvation history, not . . . an eternal vision of ultimate and unknowable mystery" (p. 69).

30. Yet it is a necessary part of the fiction that Dante be placed above the earth, as we are reminded when in the

sphere of Saturn he looks back and reports, "The little threshing-floor that makes us so fierce all appeared to me from hills to river-mouths, while I was wheeling with the eternal Twins" (Canto 22, 11. 151–153).

31. Chiarenza, p. 78.

32. Ibid., p. 81.

33. Ibid., p. 90 n. 4.

34. At the beginning of the *Paradiso* Dante is unable to look directly at the light of the sun. Beatrice can, "and as a second ray will issue from the first and mount up again, like a pilgrim that would return home, so from her action, infused by the eyes into my imagination, mine was made, and beyond our wont I fixed by eyes on the sun" (Canto 1, 11. 49–54). This process is repeated. At each stage, so long as Beatrice is with him, Dante must first see through her eyes until his own become accustomed to the intensity of light. As in *Purgatorio*, the growth and strength of his capacities of apprehension, understanding, and knowledge are developed gradually.

35. Dante is quite clearly familiar with the Scholastic view that immaterial substances can only be known by means of sensible images; cf. *S.T.* Ia. 79, 3, cited by Singleton in his notes, *Paradiso*, Part II, pp. 80–81.

36. In comparing the views of Dante and Aquinas on perception, Singleton makes an important point: "We have seen the latter noting explicitly that the truth of revelation is not shown to man that he may see it, but as expressed in words so that he may hear it. But no poet could afford to adopt such a position, and it is interesting to observe Dante declaring as much in these verses. The reference is to Canto 4, 11. 37–45. A poet, who must see (that we in turn may see), must insist that man learns only from sense experience even at these transcendent heights" (*Dante Studies II: Journey to Beatrice*, p. 25).

III: UNIVERSALS AND PARTICULARS:
FRACASTORO AND BARBARO

1. Girolamo Fracastoro, *Opera Omnia*. I use Ruth Kelso's translation of *Naugerius*. Passages from *Turrius* and *De Anima* are my translations from the second edition (Venice, 1574).

2. Hathaway, *The Age of Criticism*, p. 318. One of the many services of this book has been to draw attention to Fracastoro's effort to develop a psychology of imaginative perception, and my account is heavily indebted to Hathaway's analysis.

3. I am following Hathaway's summary, pp. 319–322.

4. Ibid., p. 322.

5. *Naugerius*, p. 59.

6. Ibid., p. 58.

7. Ibid.

8. Ibid.

9. Ibid., p. 60.

10. *Fracastorius; Opera*, pp. 151^V–152^V.

11. *Turrius; Opera*, p. 121^V.

12. See Hathaway, p. 319. He compares subnotion, the initial sorting out of sense impressions, to the modern concept of stream of consciousness. If he is correct, it would suggest that for Fracastoro these early stages of thinking occur almost simultaneously.

13. *Turrius; Opera*, p. 127^V.

14. Ibid., p. 128^r. It is useful to set this passage against Ficino's epistemology. According to Kristeller, *The Philosophy of Marsilio Ficino*, pp. 233–234, Ficino uses an Aristotelian psychology, but, although he understands the movement of mind toward the contemplation of ideas as beginning in material particulars and proceeding in an orderly way towards increasingly universal concepts, he believes that there is an absolute difference in the ways in which it understands the material or sensible on the one hand and ideas on the other. Thus Ficino says, "metaphysicians conclude that the intellect may at some time think without the images of phantasy" (*Opera Omnia*, p. 715; Kristeller's translation, pp. 226–227). Ficino thinks of the imagination and phantasy—the one presentational, the other searching out intentions—as capable only of dealing with individual things and forms (Kristeller, pp. 235–236). Thus the two modes of thought Fracastoro believes to be causally and diachronically related are for Ficino radically differentiated.

15. *Opera*, p. 128^V.

16. Ibid., p. 129^r.

17. Cicero, *Orator*, pp. 311–313. Immediately after this passage Cicero equates the idea of perfection with the Platonic theory of transcendent ideas. However, one should consult Erwin Panofsky's reminder that Cicero has substantially modified Plato and that Renaissance Neoplatonism usually understands the relationship between the natural and the conceptual in accordance with this modification. See *Idea: A Concept in Art Theory*, pp. 11–14, 53–57. He also notes that two contradictory esthetic principles dwelt side by side in the Renaissance: the mimetic imperative of fidelity to nature and the obligation to improve on nature. "On the one hand, nature could be overcome by the freely creative 'phantasy' capable of altering appearances above and beyond the possibility of natural variation and even of bringing forth completely novel creatures such as centaurs and chimeras. On the other hand, and more importantly, nature could be overcome by the artistic intellect, which—not so much by 'inventing' as by selecting and improving—can, and accordingly should, make visible a beauty never completely realized in actuality" (p. 48).

18. *Turrius; Opera*, p. 131$^\text{V}$. "Intention" is equivalent to "response."

19. *Naugerius*, p. 68.

20. Ibid., pp. 68–69. My emphasis.

21. Ibid., p. 69.

22. Ibid., pp. 69–70.

23. Ibid., p. 71.

24. *A History of Literary Criticism in the Italian Renaissance*, II, 725.

25. The text is in Bernard Weinberg, ed., *Trattati di Poetica e Retorica del Cinquecento*, 2:361. Page references are included in the text.

IV: SIDNEY'S APOLOGY FOR POETRY

1. Geoffrey Shepherd, ed., *An Apology for Poetry or Defence of Poesy*, p. 104, lines 34–37. Shepherd's introduction, which touches on a number of the issues discussed in this chapter, is useful, as are his notes. My references to the *Apology* are

incorporated in the text and designate page and line numbers in this edition.

2. The Italian interest in mimetic theory is exhaustively reviewed in Hathaway's *The Age of Criticism* and Weinberg's *A History of Literary Criticism in the Italian Renaissance*.

3. An early and influential statement from the point of view of rhetorical theory is Quintillian's in *The Institutio Oratorio*, II, 433–435: "There are certain experiences which the Greeks call φαντασιαι and the Romans *visions*, whereby things absent are presented to our imagination with such extreme vividness that they seem actually to be before our eyes. It is the man who is really sensitive to such impressions who will have the greatest power over emotions."

4. On the human scale the cosmic principle of attraction Plato treats in *Philebus* is the instinct to pleasure necessary to the preservation and extension of life. For Aristotle in *Ethica Nichomachaea* (1174b), pleasure occurs in the impression of a suitable object upon a healthy organ. He also notes a hierarchy of pleasures according to the hierarchy of the senses. Aquinas (*S.T.* Ia. 2ae. 22) suggests that we may be drawn to things by pleasure anticipated in the imagination, in other words by desire, whose fulfilment is pleasure. Renaissance discussions occur in, *inter alia*, Lorenzo Valla, *De Voluptate* (1431), *Opera Omnia*, pp. 912–952; Marsilio Ficino, *Liber de Voluptate* (1457), *Opera Omnia*, pp. 987–1012; and Philip Melancthon, *Liber de Anima*, pp. 115–119. Among these, doctrine varies—in particular Ficino locates pleasure in the God-given capacity to identify the idea behind material appearance—but they have in common the view that it begins in sensory experience, whether direct or imaginative. Aquinas notes that images in the imagination can stimulate responses similar to those that result from sensing. The point to notice is that ordinary sensory pleasure is the model for more strictly intellectual kinds.

5. Cf. Melancthon, p. 117: "Quod latet ignotum est, ignoti nulla cupido."

6. *The Poems of Sir Philip Sidney*, lines 1–3.

7. Astrophil's plan is, of course, stillborn, as the remainder

of the sonnet makes plain. But the cause of failure is his effort to use borrowed and inauthentic invention, not a mistaken theory of response.

8. Sidney writes: "That imitation whereof Poetry is, hath the most conveniency to Nature of all other, insomuch that, as Aristotle saith, those things which in themselves are horrible, as cruel battles, unnatural monsters, are made in poetical imitation delightful" (114. 5–8). The reference is to Chapter 4 of the *Poetics*. See also *Astrophil and Stella*, Sonnet 34.

9. Ludovico Castelvetro, *Poetica d'Aristotele Vulgarizzata, et Sposta*, pp. 149 (verse or melody), 71 (verisimilitude), 279–280, 295 (types of plot). In addition, he mentions the marvelous (p. 549) and the accidents of fortune (p. 29).

10. Julius Caesar Scaliger, *Poetices Libri Septem* (1561), p. 13.

11. *The Prose Works of Sir Philip Sidney,*

12. The original distinction is Plato's (*Sophist*, 235). Sidney modifies it substantially from its character as the difference between accurate and inaccurate representation to point up moral categories. Shepherd's note, *Apology*, p. 202, refers us to Mazzoni's *On the Defense of the Comedy of Dante*, which elaborates the issue considerably. Mazzoni defines icastic imitation as recording what exists or is possible and the phantastic as invented or made up, but he avoids reducing them to terms of moral value. Superficially, Sidney's view that poetic fiction never pretends to truth might be equated with Mazzoni's phantastic imitation, but his phrase "unworthy objects" suggests a very different orientation. For him the phantastic involves "wanton shows of better hidden matters" (125. 33). On Mazzoni, see Hathaway, *The Age of Criticism*, p. 120.

13. Sidney asks, "What child is there that, coming to a play, and seeing *Thebes* written in great letters upon an old door, doth believe that it is Thebes?" (124. 17–19). But later he criticizes *Gorbuduc* for just such a device (134. 13–25). O. B. Hardison, Jr., "The Two Voices of Sidney's *Apology for Poetry*," is an able discussion of the contradiction.

14. Sidney argues that readers respond most powerfully to the poet's "pictures [of] what should be . . . ; so in Poesy looking but for fiction, they shall use the narration but as an

imaginative ground-plot of a profitable invention" (124. 21, 25–27).

15. Cf. *Apology*, 107. 28–31, 120. 25–28.

16. He seems at best a cautious Platonist. Sonnets 5 and 25 incorporate a version of Platonic idealism: in each case the operative value of the concept is presented for witty refutation. The *Apology*, 128. 8–130. 10, has an extensive discussion of Plato's attitude toward poets, concluding that he sought to banish only those who abused the art. For those critics who argue that Sidney is a philosophic Platonist there is his account of Menenius Agrippa's homely and persuasive fable about the civil war between the head and the belly set against "far fetched maxims of Philosophy, which (especially if they were Platonic) they must have learned geometry before they could well have conceived . . ." (115. 3–5).

17. See Shepherd's note, p. 156, and chapter 3 above.

18. Forrest G. Robinson, *The Shape of Things Known: Sidney's "Apology" in Its Philosophic Tradition*, understands Sidney's *Idea*, and indeed his whole theory of affect, quite differently, arguing that Sidney's concept of "picture" is not "an art of language in which there is a premium on vivid descriptions of external nature" but "an abstraction, a concept made visible to the reader's mind" (p. 99). In the poet's mind the poem is "a kind of mental vision" that becomes "a diagrammatic concept, a mental chart upon which the 'reasons' of a poem are organized" (p. 118). The major difficulty with this reading is that it lends Sidney's theory a rationalistic emphasis that seems to me unsupported by the text. Sidney maintains that naked precept is neither initially attractive nor ultimately moving, but Robinson confines delight (and, I assume, the moving power of poetry) to what he calls "the carefully erected veneer of verbal particulars" (p. 122).

19. See also 108. 37–109. 7, where Sidney points out that the story of Dives and Lazarus is more effective than "moral commonplaces" because it "more constantly (as it were) inhabit[s] both memory and judgment."

20. He makes the same point earlier: "For indeed Poetry ever setteth virtue so out in her best colours, making Fortune

her well-waiting handmaid, that one must needs be enamoured of her" (111. 26–29).

21. Emphasis on appeal to the emotions is especially important in rhetorical and oratorical theory, and Sidney adapts this point of view to poetics even more persistently than Fracastoro or Barbaro. It is also emphasized in the early stages of Humanism. In one of his letters Salutati remarks that verbal ornament joined to gravity of idea moves the soul pleasurably and powerfully (*Epistolario*, I, 23); Streuver, commenting on this letter, says ". . . action is the product of the soul, not just the intellect, and the only way to transform an idea into action is through affecting the senses, the imagination as well as the reason; form is the only recourse" (*The Language of History in the Renaissance*, p. 59). See also Henry Peacham, *The Garden of Eloquence*, sig. A3: ". . . how wonderfully shall his [the orator's] perswasions take place in the minds of men, and his wordes pearce into their inward partes? For by Fygures, as it were by sundry streames, that great & forcible floud of Eloquence . . . the Oratour may leade his hearers which way he list, and draw them to what affection he will. . . ."

22. Shepherd, p. 182, records instances of the belief in natural reason from Plutarch to Castiglione, Amyot, and Hooker. Sidney states the doctrine rather baldly.

23. "Wit" and "conceit" are notoriously flexible terms in general and in the *Apology*. They may refer specifically to reason or intelligence or more loosely to the cooperative functions of several faculties, with emphasis on inventing, making up, or feigning. See Shepherd's excellent note to 104. 3 on p. 166.

24. Harry Berger, Jr., "The Renaissance Imagination: Second World and Green World," p. 43.

V: VERISIMILAR THINGS: TASSO'S
DISCOURSES ON THE HEROIC POEM

1. Cf. Hardison, "The Two Voices of Sidney's *Apology for Poetry*."

2. *Discorsi del Arte Poetica* in *Prose*, p. 351.

3. Ibid., pp. 351–352.

4. Castelvetro, *Poetica d'Aristotele Vulgarizzata, et Sposta,* p. 29.

5. Ibid., p. 30.

6. Ibid., p. 109. Scaliger was the first to derive a firm doctrine of the unities from Aristotle.

7. Ibid., pp. 121–122. Estimates of the intelligence of the audience were variable and usually less condescending than Castelvetro's. For example, Francesco Buonamici, whose *Discorsi . . . in Difesa d'Aristotele* (1597), according to Weinberg, "ranks as one of the best works on the *Poetics* of the century" (*A History of Literary Criticism in the Italian Renaissance*, II, 699), thinks the audience somewhat more perceptive. They are aware, for one thing, of the difference between fiction and fact; therefore Buonamici attempts to relate unity of plot, its suspenses, and its complications to theories of pleasure which are less bound by time and custom. At the same time, for reasons other than those of Castelvetro, he demands veri-similitude: ". . . there is a certain power in words and in actions which, as they reveal passion and character, always move the listener; and as they move him, they persuade him, since every man readily believes what he would wish" (Weinberg's translation, II, 697–698).

8. *Discourses on the Heroic Poem* (1594), p. 5. Subsequent quotations and references to this translation will be noted in my text.

9. *Prose*, p. 355.

10. My discussion of Tasso passes over his part in the lengthy debate over the meaning of *catharsis*. The subject receives a full and excellent survey in Hathaway's *The Age of Criticism*, pp. 205–300. Among other issues of controversy (for example, whether purgation was a homeopathic or allopathic process), some Renaissance critics extended the general cathartic principle to genres other than tragedy, assigning, as Tasso does, different forms of affect to different kinds of poem. See Hathaway, pp. 291–300. One result of Hathaway's discussion is to emphasize that different critics found different sources for esthetic pleasure, some, such as Castelvetro, in recognition (p. 236), others, such as Piccolimini, in the release from fear (pp. 243–244), and still others, such as Giacomini, in

the experiencing of emotion (p. 254). Tasso, as Hathaway notes (p. 260), is inclined to regard the proper degree of emotive response as moderate. Cf. *Del Giudizio sovra la Sua Gerusalemme* in *Prose Diverse*, I, 536–547. More generally Tasso associates esthetic pleasure with the manner of artistic presentation.

11. Tasso covers himself sufficiently to say, "So too Plutarch in his book on interpreting poetry teaches us that the poet may rightly express blame and interpose his judgement, censuring wickedness and thus showing us what is useful; otherwise he might harm us with the example of the thing he imitates" (p. 87). This is in contrast to Sidney's confidence in the teaching power of the example by itself; see, for example, p. 108 in Shepherd's edition of the *Apology*.

12. Like some other Renaissance critics Tasso tends to confuse *enargeia* with *energeia*, calling the former "energy" and yet describing it correctly as "the power that makes us behold the things narrated" (p. 189, and again, p. 192). In distinguishing the styles of Homer and Virgil, he says that Homer "sets things more vividly before our eyes and particularizes them more," which is *enargeia* (pp. 194–195). Annabel M. Patterson, *Hermogenes and the Renaissance: Seven Ideas of Style*, pp. 131–133, discusses the misconceptions of both Tasso and Sidney, noting that for Tasso *energeia* is the term applied to the means by which the poet makes things both seen and heard. As she also mentions, for the Greeks *enargeia* means clarity or brightness, while *energeia* refers to action or energy. See also Neil Rudenstine, *Sidney's Poetic Development*, pp. 149–171, as well as Robinson's objections to Rudenstine in *The Shape of Things Known*, pp. 128–135. Jean Hagstrum, *The Sister Arts: The Tradition of Literary Pictorialism and English Poetry from Dryden to Gray*, p. 11, says that in rhetoric *enargeia* "was used to describe the power that verbal visual imagery possessed in setting before the hearer the very object or scene being described." But when it comes to *energeia* Hagstrum says that Aristotle uses the term to describe the effect of setting "things before the eyes of the auditor by using words that signify actuality" (p. 12). Hagstrum then sees *energeia* as "the actualization of potency, the realization of capacity or capability, the

achievement in art and rhetoric of the dynamic and purposive life of nature."

13. Compare this passage with the simpler statement from the *Discorsi del Arte Poetica* at the beginning of this chapter.

14. There is a complicated background to Tasso's strong remarks: he was deeply involved in a quarrel over the relative merits of his own and Ariosto's work; see Weinberg, *History of Literary Criticism in the Italian Renaissance*, II, 954–1073; and Hathaway, *The Age of Criticism*, pp. 390–396.

15. Hathaway's *The Age of Criticism*, pp. 355–389, deals subtly and fully with the issues involved.

16. Mazzoni, *On the Defense of the Comedy of Dante*, pp. 47–48.

17. Ibid., p. 42.

18. Ibid., p. 60. Mazzoni's procedure is to move systematically through a series of linked definitions of poetry considered in various modes; his poetics thus frequently has the appearance of cool analysis, but his final definition (p. 81) becomes prescriptive.

19. Hathaway, *The Age of Criticism*, p. 394, refers to Aquinas on this point. The indivisible mind is pure intellect. The divisible intellect is lower and thinks serially according to proof, demonstration, example; cf. *S.T.* 1a. 1. 9. Giordano Bruno equates the divisible mind with the potential, possible, or passive intellect, and the indivisible mind with the active intellect. The one "is informed according to an infinity of degrees and an infinity of natural forms" and is "frenzied, wandering, and uncertain. . . ." The other puts man in touch with universal intelligence; *Giordano Bruno's The Heroic Frenzies*, First Part, 5th dialogue, p. 155. Aristotle deals rather differently with this distinction in Book III of *De Anima*.

20. *Prose Diverse*, I, 528.

21. Words and their meanings, like manners and customs, are man-made and variable for Tasso; see p. 73. Buonamici, *Discorsi . . . in Difesa di Aristotile*, p. 105, states the issue more lucidly: "The Philosophers have taught about signs and similitudes that similitudes are natural and signs depend on our will; that since similitudes are natural, they do not change according to what a man does; that a species does not appear

in my imagination with the same delineation and colors which are in me; but that when I signify a thing with one meaning or another, it is according to human choice." Hence, what is represented and the means of representation are different things, even though what is represented is perceived in the imagination as a similitude. This reasoning is part of Buonamici's argument against Castelvetro's belief that the means of representation—as in the units of time—must be as close as possible to the thing represented.

22. Like some of Dante's Renaissance commentators, Tasso (p. 33) interprets his references in *Purgatorio* 17 and *Paradiso* 33 to the phantasy as indicating a concept of the intellectual imagination.

VI: CONCLUSION

1. F. M. Padelford, *Select Translations from Scaliger's Poetics* (New York, 1905), p. 2.

2. Herschel Baker, *The Image of Man*, p. 242. See also Edgar Wind, *Pagan Mysteries in the Renaissance*, p. 191.

3. *The Image of Man*, pp. 244—245. The second sentence might serve to epitomize Dante's position, but as Baker points out, some Neoplatonists from Pico to Milton virtually abandoned the doctrine of original sin in their enthusiasm over the power of human reason to achieve such knowledge and such a vision.

4. Marsilio Ficino, *Five Questions Concerning the Mind*, pp. 203, 205—206.

5. Giordano Bruno, *The Heroic Frenzies (De Gli Eroici Furori)* (1585), Second Part, 2nd dialogue, p. 226.

6. Ibid., Second Part, 3rd dialogue, p. 229.

7. Ibid., First Part, 4th dialogue, pp. 131—133.

8. Ibid., "The Argument of the Nolan," p. 63.

9. Henry Reynolds, *Mythomystes* I, 143, 169, and passim.

10. Thomas Carew, "An Elegie upon the death of the Dean of Pauls, Dr. John Donne," *The Poems of Thomas Carew*, lines 15—20.

11. George Chapman, "To My Deare and Most Worthy

Friend Master Mathew Roydon," *The Poems of George Chapman*, p. 19.

12. Ibid., p. 49. Chapman's position is reiterated at greater length in the poem addressed to M. Harriots, accompanying *Achilles Shield*; pp. 181–185.

13. *The Age of Criticism*, p. 206.

14. Ibid., pp. 212–213.

15. Agnolo Segni, *Ragionamenti sopra le Cose Pertinenti alla Poetica*, p. 43. Cf. Hathaway, *The Age of Criticism*, pp. 249–250. Weinberg has printed a much expanded version of Segni's lectures as *Lezioni intorno alla Poesia* in *Trattati di Poetica e Retorica del Cinquecento*, vol. 3. For Segni's extended discussion of purgation and affect, see esp. pp. 68–84.

16. *Ragionamenti*, p. 45.

17. Thomas Hobbes, *Leviathan*, p. 23. He adds that "imagination and memory are but one thing," by which he means that imagination, especially the compounding or fictionalizing kind, is really the result of experience and recollection. It gives rise to appetite or passion, and although Hobbes may seem in this respect to echo traditional psychology, there are important differences. In contrast to Aquinas's view that appetite is "natural," Hobbes sees it as the result of experience. Moreover, as against the Neoplatonic concept of pleasure or contentment in the contemplation of the permanent and unchanging, Hobbes derives them from agitation, motion, or proceeding. Finally, it must be said that any point of resemblance between Hobbes and Italian Baroque theorists is probably fortuitous; yet both reflect the general tendency of the period to question the connections between mental faculties and the real or certain. For a detailed view of Hobbes as literary theorist see Clarence DeWitt Thorpe, *The Aesthetic Theory of Thomas Hobbes: With Special Reference to His Contribution to the Psychological Approach in English Literary Criticism*, pp. 92, 135, and passim.

18. *Leviathan*, p. 27.

19. Matteo Peregrini, *Delle Acutezze, Che Altrimenti Spiriti, Vivezze e Concetti Volgarmente Si Appellano* (1639), in Ezio Raimondi, ed., *Trattatisti e Narratori del Seicento*, p. 122.

20. Sforza Pallavicino, *Del Bene Libri Quattro* (1644), in

August Buck, Klaus Heitmann, and Walter Mettman, eds. *Dichtungslehren der Romania aus der Zeit der Renaissance und des Barock*, pp. 228–229.

21. Ibid., p. 229.

22. Ibid.

23. Eugenio Donato, "Tesauro's Poetics: Through the Looking Glass," p. 17.

24. Emanuele Tesauro, *Il Cannocchiale Aristotelico o Sia Idea dell'Arguta et Ingeniosa Elocutione* . . . (1655), pp. 82–83. Donato's explanation of Tesauro's theory is important. He emphasizes ("Tesauro's Poetics," pp. 21–25) the independence of the "reality" created by the poet's metaphor, its visual expressiveness and theatricality, and its quality of order imposed upon nature from the pleasures of wit. Such autonomy, according to Donato (p. 26), substitutes an invented world for a given: "A poetic of 'correspondence' can only exist in a previously ordered universe, but as we have seen, the function of Tesauro's metaphor is precisely to order the universe, and when either Tesauro or Marino uses a metaphor that at one time had significance in a system allowing for 'correspondences,' it is always in a negative way."

25. Edmund Spenser, "A Letter of the Authors Expounding the Whole Intention in the course of this Worke . . .," in Dodge, ed., *The Complete Poetical Works* of *Spenser*, p. 136.

26. Hathaway entitles a chapter in *The Age of Criticism*, "Tasso's Magic Realism."

27. "The Answer of Mr. Hobbes to Sr Will. D'Avenant's Preface Before *Gondibert*," in Spingarn, ed., *Critical Essays of the Seventeenth Century*, II, 59.

Bibliography

Adams, Hazard, ed. *Critical Theory Since Plato*. Harcourt Brace Jovanovich, New York: 1971.

Albertus Magnus. *Opera Omnia*. 38 vols. Paris, 1890–1899; *De Anima, De Apprehensione, & Liber de Natura et Origine Animae*, vol. 5.

———. *Textus Triorum Libriorum De Anima Aristotelis cum Commentario Doctrinus Veneralibus Domini Alberti Magni*. Cologne, 1491.

Allers, Rudolph. "St. Augustine's Doctrine on Illumination." *Franciscan Studies*, n.s. 12 (1952):27–46.

Aquinas, Thomas. *Summa contra Gentiles*. Trans. Anton C. Pegis. New York, 1955.

———. *Summa Theologiae*. 60 vols. New York and London, 1963.

Aristotle. *Aristotle's* De Anima *in the Version of William of Moerbeke and the Commentary of St. Thomas Aquinas*. Trans. Kenelm Foster and Silvester Humphries. New Haven: Yale University Press, 1951.

———. *The Basic Works of Aristotle*. Ed. and trans. Richard McKeon. New York: Random House, 1941.

———. *The Works of Aristotle*. Trans. under the editorship of

J. A. Smith . . . W. D. Ross. 12 vols. Oxford: Oxford University Press, 1908–1952: *De Memoria et Reminiscentia*. Trans. J. I. Beare; *De Rhetorica*. Trans. W. Rhys Roberts; *De Somnis*. Trans. J. I. Beare.

Atkins, J. W. *English Literary Criticism: The Renascence*. New York: Barnes and Noble; London: Methuen, 1968.

Augustine. *De Genesi ad Litteram*. Ed. Josephus Zycha. *Corpus Scriptorum Ecclesiastorum Latinorum*. vol. 28. Vienna, 1884; repr. New York and London, 1970.

———. *Letters*. Vol. 1. Trans. Sister Wilfrid Parsons. Washington, D.C., 1951.

———. *On Christian Doctrine*. Trans. D. W. Robertson, Jr. New York: Liberal Arts Press, 1958.

———. *The Trinity*. Trans. Stephen McKenna. Washington, D.C., 1963.

Bacon, Francis. *Advancement of Learning*. Everyman ed. London: J. M. Dent, 1945.

Baker, Herschel. *The Image of Man: A Study of the Idea of Human Dignity in Classical Antiquity, the Middle Ages, and The Renaissance*. New York: Harper and Brothers, 1967; 1st publ. as *The Dignity of Man*. Cambridge, Mass.: Harvard University Press, 1947.

Barbaro, Daniele. *Della Eloquenza* (1557); repr. in *Trattati di Poetica e Retorica del Cinquecento*. Ed. Bernard Weinberg. Vol. 2. Bari: Gius. Laterza & Figli, 1970.

Berger, Harry, Jr. "The Renaissance Imagination: Second World and Green World." *Centennial Review* 9 (1965): 36–78.

Bergin, Thomas. *Dante*. Boston: Houghton Mifflin Company, 1965.

Boccaccio, Giovanni. *Boccaccio on Poetry*. Ed. and trans. C. G. Osgood. New York: Liberal Arts Press, 1956; 1st publ. Princeton: Princeton University Press, 1930.

Bonaventure. *The Mind's Road to God*. Trans. George Boas. New York: Liberal Arts Press, 1953.

Bruno, Giordano. *Giordano Bruno's The Heroic Frenzies*. Ed. and trans. Paul Eugene Memmo, Jr. Chapel Hill: University of North Carolina Press, 1964.

Buck, August; Heitmann, Klaus; Metmann, Walter, eds. *Dichtungs-lehren der Romania aus der Renaissance und des Barok*. Frankfurt am Main, 1972.

Bundy, Murray W. *The Theory of Imagination in Classical and Mediaeval Thought*. University of Illinois Studies in Language and Literature, vol. 12, nos. 2–3. Urbana, 1927.

Buonamici, Francesco. *Discorsi Poetici nella Accademia Fiorentina in Difesa d'Aristotile*. Florence, 1597.

Carew, Thomas. *The Poems of Thomas Carew*. Ed. Rhodes Dunlap. Oxford: Oxford University Press, 1957.

Castelvetro, Ludovico. *Poetica d'Aristotile Vulgarizzata, et Sposta*. Vienna, 1570; 2d ed. Basle, 1576.

Chapman, George. *The Poems of George Chapman*. Ed. Phyllis Brooks Bartlett. New York, 1941; repr. 1962.

Chiarenza, Marguerite Mills. "The Imageless Vision and Dante's *Paradiso*." *Dante Studies* 90 (1972): Harvard University Press; 77–91.

Cicero. *De Oratore*. Loeb ed. 2 vols. Cambridge, Mass.: Harvard University Press, London: William Heinemann Ltd.; 1960.

―――. *Orator*. Trans. H. M. Hubbell. Loeb ed. Cambridge, Mass.: Harvard University Press; London: William Heinemann Ltd., 1952.

Copleston, F. L. *A History of Medieval Philosophy*. London, 1972.

―――. *A History of Philosophy*: Vol 2. *Mediaeval Philosophy: Augustine to Scotus*. New York: Doubleday and Co., 1960.

Costa, Dennis John. "Dante as a Poet-Theologian." *Dante Studies* 89 (1971):61–72.

Daniello, Bernardino. *Dante con l'Espositione di M. Bernardino Daniello*. Venice, 1568.

Dante Alighieri. *Convivio*. Trans. W. W. Jackson. Oxford: Oxford University Press, 1909.

―――. *Dante's Vita Nuova: A Translation and an Essay*. Trans. Mark Musa. New Edition. Bloomington: Indiana University Press, 1973.

———. *De Vulgari Eloquentia* and *Epistolae*. A Translation of the Latin Works of Dante Alighieri. Temple Classics ed. London: J. M. Dent & Sons, 1904.

———. *The Divine Comedy: Paradiso*. Ed. and trans. C. S. Singleton. 2 vols. Princeton: Princeton University Press, 1975.

———. *The Divine Comedy: Purgatorio*. Ed. and trans. C. S. Singleton. 2 vols. Princeton: Princeton University Press, 1973.

———. *Il Convivio*. Ed. G. Busnelli and G. Vandelli. 2 vols. Florence, 1968.

DeMaria, Robert, Jr. "The Ideal Reader: A Critical Fiction." *PMLA* 93 (1978):463–473.

Donato, Eugenio. "Tesauro's Poetics: Through the Looking Glass." *MLN* 78 (1963):15–30.

Ficino, Marsilio. *Five Questions Concerning the Mind* (1495). Trans. Josephine L. Burroughs. In *The Renaissance Philosophy of Man*. Eds. Ernst Cassirer, Paul Otto Kristeller, and John Herman Randall, Jr. Chicago: University of Chicago Press, 1948.

———. *Opera Omnia*. Basle, 1561.

Fracastoro, Girolamo. *Naugerius*. Trans. Ruth Kelso. University of Illinois Studies in Language and Literature, vol. 9, no. 3. Urbana, 1924.

———. *Opera Omnia*. Venice, 1555; 2d ed. 1574.

Gilson, Etienne. *The Philosophy of St. Thomas Aquinas*. Trans. Edward Bullough. Cambridge, 1924.

Gray, Hanna, "Renaissance Humanism: The Pursuit of Eloquence," *JHI* 24 (1963): 497–514.

Hagstrum, Jean. *The Sister Arts: The Tradition of Literary Pictorialism and English Poetry from Dryden to Gray*. Chicago: University of Chicago Press, 1958.

Hardison, O. B., Jr. *The Enduring Monument: A Study of the Idea of Praise in Renaissance Literary Theory and Practice*. Chapel Hill: University of North Carolina Press, 1962.

———. "The Two Voices of Sidney's *Apology for Poetry*." *ELR*, 2, no. 2 (1972):83–99.

Harvey, E. Ruth. *The Inward Wits: Psychological Theory in the Middle Ages and the Renaissance*. Warburg Institute

Surveys, 6. London, 1975.

Hathaway, Baxter. *The Age of Criticism: The Late Renaissance in Italy*. Ithaca: Cornell University Press, 1962.

Hobbes, Thomas. "The Answer of Mr. Hobbes to Sr. Will. D'Avenant's Preface before *Gondibert*" (1650). *Critical Essays of the Seventeenth Century*. Ed. J. E. Spingarn. 3 vols. Oxford: Oxford University Press, 1970; repr. Bloomington: Indiana University Press, 1957. 2:54–67.

———. *Leviathan, or the Matter, Forme, and Power of a Commonwealth Ecclesiastical and Civil* (1651). Ed. Michael Oakeshott. New York: Collier Books, 1962.

Kristeller, Paul Oskar. *The Philosophy of Marsilio Ficino*. Cambridge, Mass., 1964; 1st publ. in English, 1934.

———. *Renaissance Thought: The Classic, Scholastic, and Humanistic Strains*. New York: Harper & Brothers, 1955.

Landino, Christoforo. *Dante con l'Espositione . . . de . . . Landino*. Venice, 1564.

Levi, Anthony. *French Moralists: The Theory of the Passions, 1585 to 1649*. Oxford: Oxford University Press, 1964.

Longinus. *On The Sublime*. Trans. W. R. Roberts. In *Critical Theory Since Plato*. Ed. Hazard Adams. New York: Harcourt Brace Jovanovich, 1971.

MacCaffrey, Isabel G. *Spenser's Allegory: The Anatomy of Imagination*. Princeton: Princeton University Press, 1976.

Mazzoni, Jacopo. *On the Defense of the Comedy of Dante*. Part I, Cesena, 1587; Parts I and II, 1688.

Melancthon, Philip. *Liber de Anima*. Wittenberg, 1553; 1st publ. 1540.

Murrin, Michael. *The Veil of Allegory: Some Notes toward a Theory of Allegorical Rhetoric in the English Renaissance*. Chicago: University of Chicago Press, 1969.

Nash, Ronald H. *The Light of the Mind: St. Augustine's Theory of Knowledge*. Lexington: University of Kentucky Press, 1969.

Newman, Francis X. "St. Augustine's Three Visions and the Structure of the *Commedia*." *MLN* 82 (1967):56–76.

Pallavicino, Sforza. *Del Bene Libri Quattro*. Rome, 1644. In

Dichtungslehren der Romania aus der Zeit der Renaissance und das Barok. Eds. August Buck et al. Frankfurt am Main, 1972.

Panofsky, Erwin. *Idea: A Concept in Art Theory*. Trans. J. S. Peake. Columbia: University of South Carolina Press, 1968.

Patterson, Annabel M. *Hermogenes and the Renaissance: Seven Ideas of Style*. Princeton: Princeton University Press, 1970.

Peacham, Henry. *The Garden of Eloquence*. London, 1577.

Peregrini, Matteo. *Della Acutezze, Che Altrimenti Spiriti, Vivezza e Concetti Volgarmente Si Appellano*. Genoa, 1639. In *Trattatisti e Narratori del Seicento*. Ed. Ezio Raimondi. Milan and Naples, 1960.

Pico della Mirandola, Gianfrancesco. *On the Imagination: The Latin Text with an Introduction, an English Translation, and Notes*. Ed. and trans. Harry Caplan. Cornell Studies in English, 16. New Haven and London, 1930.

Plato. *The Dialogues of Plato*. Trans. Benjamin Jowett. 2 vols. New York: Random House, Inc., 1937.

————. *The Republic*. Trans. Paul Shorey. Loeb ed. 2 vols. Cambridge, Mass.: Harvard University Press; London: William Heinemann Ltd: 1935.

————. *The Republic of Plato*. Trans. F. M. Cornford. New York and London, 1945.

Plotinus. *The Enneads*. Trans. Stephen McKenna. 3d ed. London, 1962; 1st publ. 1927–1930.

Preminger, Alex; Hardison, O. B., Jr.; Kerrane, Kevin, eds. *Classical and Medieval Literary Criticism: Translations and Interpretations*. New York: Frederick Ungar Publishing Co., 1974.

Proclus. "Proclus on the More Difficult Questions in the *Republic*: The Nature of Poetic Art." Trans. Thomas Taylor. *In Classical and Medieval Literary Criticism*. Eds. Alex Preminger et al. New York: Frederick Ungar Publishing Co., 1974.

Quintillian. *The Institutio Oratorio*. Trans. H. E. Butler. Loeb ed. 4 vols. Cambridge, Mass.: Harvard University Press; London: William Heinemann Ltd., 1920–1922.

Rahman, F. *Avicenna's Psychology*. Oxford: Oxford University Press, 1952.

Raimondi, Ezio, ed. *Trattatisti e Narratori del Seicento*. Milan and Naples, 1960.

Reynolds, Henry. *Mythomystes*. In *Critical Essays of the Seventeenth Century*, vol. 1. Ed. J. E. Spingarn. Bloomington: Indiana University Press, 1957.

Richards, I. A. *Principles of Literary Criticism*. London: Routledge and Kegan Paul Ltd., 1925.

Robinson, Forrest G. *The Shape of Things Known: Sidney's "Apology" in Its Philosophical Tradition*. Cambridge, Mass.: Harvard University Press, 1972.

Rossky, William. "Imagination in the English Renaissance: Psychology and Poetic." *Studies in the Renaissance* 5 (1958):49–73.

Rudenstine, Neil. *Sidney's Poetic Development*. Cambridge, Mass.: Harvard University Press, 1967.

Salutati, Coluccio. *De Laboribus Herculis*. Ed. B. L. Ullman. Zurich, 1951.

———. *Epistolario di Coluccio Salutati*. Ed. F. Novati. 4 vols. Rome, 1891–1911.

Scaliger, Julius Caesar. *Poetices Libri Septem* (1561). Trans. F. M. Padelford. New York, 1904.

Schüling, Hermann. *Bibliographie der Psychologischen Literatur des 16. Jahrhunderts*. Hildesheim: Georg Olms Verlagsbuchhandlung, 1967.

Segni, Agnolo. *Lezzioni intorno alla Poesia*. In *Trattati di Poetica e Retorica del Cinquecento*, vol. 3. Ed. Bernard Weinberg. Bari: Gius, Laterza e Figli, 1972.

———. *Ragionamenti sopra le Cose Pertinenti alla Poetica*. Florence, 1581.

Seigel, Jerrold E. *Rhetoric and Philosophy in Renaissance Humanism: The Union of Wisdom and Eloquence, Petrarch to Valla*. Princeton: Princeton University Press, 1968.

Sidney, Sir Philip. *An Apology for Poetry*. Ed. Geoffrey Shepherd. London: Thomas Nelson and Sons, 1965.

———. *The Countess of Pembroke's Arcadia: The Old Arcadia*. Ed. Jean Robertson. Oxford: Oxford University Press, 1973.

————. *The Poems of Sir Philip Sidney.* Ed. William A. Ringler, Jr. Oxford: Oxford University Press, 1962.

————. *The Prose Works of Sir Philip Sidney.* Ed. Albert Feuillerat. 4 vols. Cambridge: Cambridge University Press, 1912; repr. 1962–1963.

Singleton, C. S. *Dante Studies II: Journey to Beatrice.* Cambridge, Mass.: Harvard University Press, 1958.

————. *An Essay on the "Vita Nuova."* Cambridge, Mass.: Harvard University Press, 1958.

Spenser, Edmund. *The Complete Poetical Works of Edmund Spenser.* Ed. R. E. Neil Dodge. Cambridge, Mass.: Houghton Mifflin Company, 1908.

Spingarn, J. E., ed. *Critical Essays of the Seventeenth Century.* 3 vols. Oxford: Oxford University Press, 1907; repr. Bloomington: Indiana University Press, 1957.

————. *A History of Literary Criticism in the Renaissance.* New York: Harcourt, Brace & World, 1963.

Struever, Nancy S. *The Language of History in the Renaissance: Rhetoric and Historical Consciousness in Florentine Humanism.* Princeton: Princeton University Press, 1970.

Swing, T. K. *The Fragile Leaves of the Sybil: Dante's Master Plan.* Westminster, Md.: The Newman Press, 1962.

Tasso, Torquato. *Del Giudizio sovra la Sua Gerusalemme.* In *Prose Diverse.* Ed. Cesare Guasti. 2 vols. Florence, 1875.

————. *Discorsi del Arte Poetica e in Particolare sopra il Poema Eroico.* Venice, 1587.

————. *Discourses on the Heroic Poem.* Trans. Mariella Cavalchini and Irene Samuel. Oxford: Oxford University Press, 1973.

————. *Prose.* Ed. Ettore Mazzali. Milan and Naples, 1959.

Tesauro, Emanuele. *Il Cannocchiale Aristotelico o Sia Idea dell' Arguta et Ingeniosa Elocutione . . .* (1655). Turin, 1670. Ed. August Buck. Bad Hamburg, Berlin, and Zurich, 1968.

Thorpe, Clarence De Witt. *The Aesthetic Theory of Thomas Hobbes: With Special Reference to His Contribution to the Psychological Approach in English Literary Criticism.* University of Michigan Publications in Language and

Literature, 18. Ann Arbor: University of Michigan Press, 1940.

Trimpi, Wesley. "The Ancient Hypothesis of Fiction: An Essay on the Origins of Literary Theory." *Traditio* 27 (1971): 1–78.

———. "The Quality of Fiction: The Rhetorical Transmission of Literary Theory." *Traditio* 30 (1974):1–118.

Trinkaus, Charles. *In Our Image and Likeness: Humanity and Divinity in Italian Humanist Thought.* 2 vols. Chicago: University of Chicago Press, 1970.

Trissino, Giorgio. *La Poetica* (1529). In *Trattati di Poetica e Retorica del Cinquecento,* vols. 1 and 2. Ed. Bernard Weinberg. Bari: Gius. Laterza e Figli, 1970–1972.

Valla, Lorenzo. *De Voluptate* (1431). In *Opera Omnia.* Basle, 1540.

Vellutello, Alessandro. *La Comedia di Dante con la Nova Espositione di Alessandro Vellutello.* Vinegia, 1544; also in Landino ed.

Vives, Juan Luis. *De Anima et Vita.* Basle, 1538; also in *Opera Omnia* (1745). 7 vols. Repr. London, 1964. Vol. 3.

Weinberg, Bernard. *A History of Literary Criticism in the Italian Renaissance.* 2 vols. Chicago: University of Chicago Press, 1961.

Weinberg, Bernard, ed. *Trattati di Poetica e Retorica del Cinquecento.* 3 vols. Bari: Gius. Laterza e Figli: 1970–1972.

Wicksteed, Philip H. *Dante and Aquinas.* New York, 1971; 1st publ. 1913.

Wimsatt, W. K., Jr., and Brooks, Cleanth. *Literary Criticism: A Short History.* New York: Random House, 1957; repr. 1967.

Wimsatt, William K., and Beardsley, Monroe C. *The Verbal Icon.* New York: The Noonday Press, 1958; first publ. 1954.

Wind, Edgar. *Pagan Mysteries in the Renaissance.* Harmondsworth, Middlesex: Penguin Books Ltd., 1967.

Index